SUBTLE STRENGTH

GORDINE

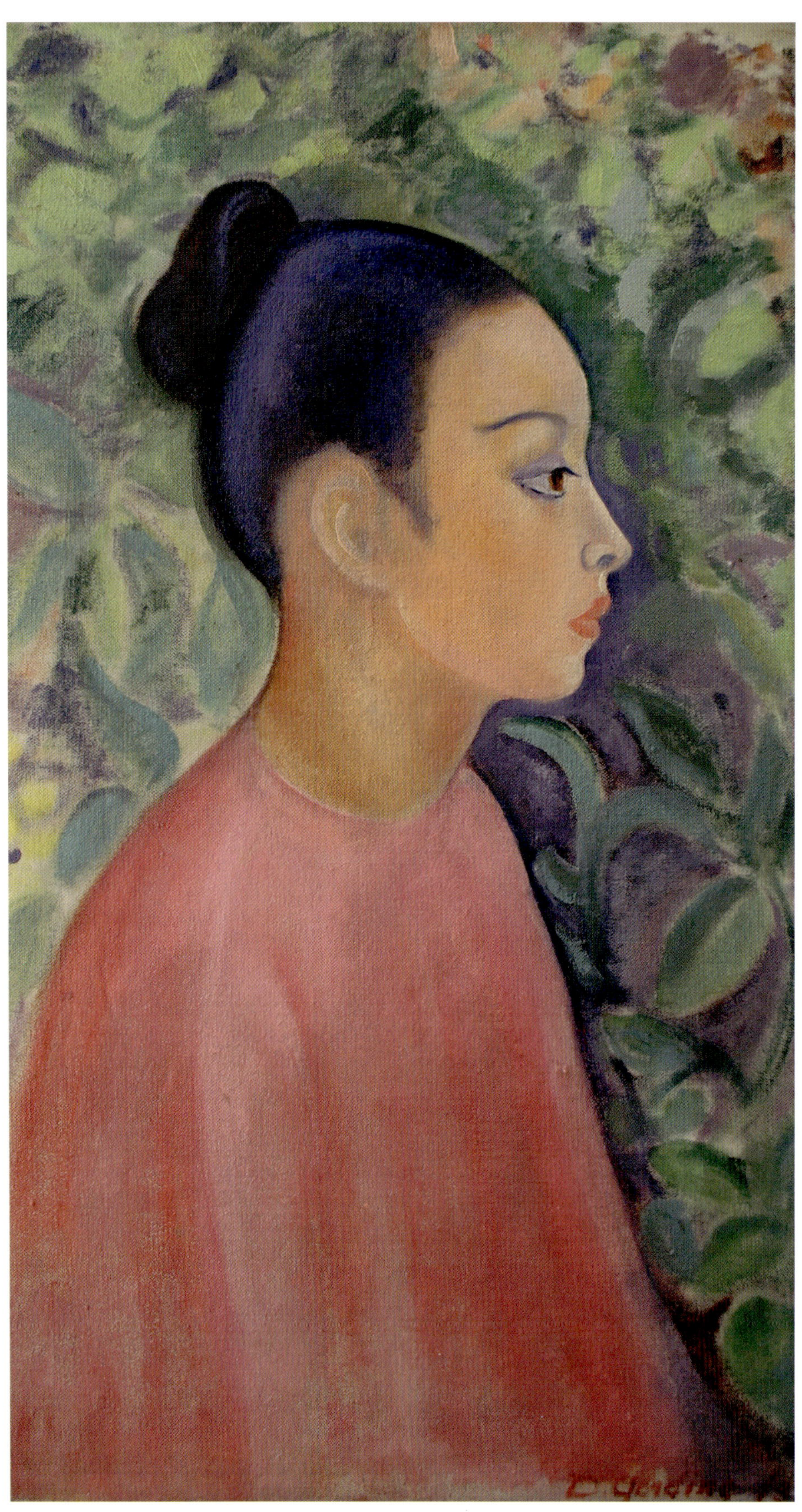

SUBTLETY AND STRENGTH

THE DRAWINGS OF DORA GORDINE

JONATHAN BLACK

and

FRAN LLOYD

Dorich House Museum, Kingston University
in association with
Philip Wilson Publishers

Published to complement the exhibition
'Dora Gordine: Sculptor, Artist, Designer'
at Dorich House, Kingston University (11
February–22 March 2009) and Kingston
Museum, Kingston upon Thames (11
February–2 May 2009).

First published in 2009 by
Philip Wilson Publishers
109 Drysdale Street
The Timber Yard
London N1 6ND
www.philip-wilson.co.uk

Distributed throughout the world (excluding
North America) by
I.B. Tauris & Co. Ltd
6 Salem Road, London W2 4BU

Distributed in North America by
Palgrave Macmillan,
a division of St Martin's Press
175 Fifth Avenue, New York NY 10010

ISBN 978-0-85667-675-8

Edited by David Hawkins

Designed by Caroline and Roger Hillier
The Old Chapel Graphic Design
www.theoldchapellivinghoe.com

Printed and bound in China by Everbest

ACKNOWLEDGEMENTS

The authors wish to offer their sincere thanks to the following individuals and institutions for the generous help they provided during the completion of this book:
Philip Athill (Abbott & Holder, London); Fine Art Society, London; Matthew Hartley; David Hawkins; Stuart Hillcock; Caroline and Roger Hillier; Chris Kennington; Kathy Lazenbatt (Royal Asiatic Society, London); Brenda Martin (Kingston University); Rupert Mass; William Neuhaus (Archives and Special Collections, University of New York at Buffalo); Emily Peters (Henry Moore Foundation Archive, Much Hadham); Gordon Samuel (Osborne Samuel Ltd, London); Tate Britain, London; Christopher Thomas (Kingston University); Ben Uri Gallery, The London Jewish Museum of Art; Magnus von Wistinghausen; Dr Jon Wood (Henry Moore Institute for the Study of Sculpture, Leeds).

Front cover: *Standing Malay Male* (detail), c. 1931–32, charcoal on paper, 66 × 56 cm, Dorich House Museum

Back cover: *Malay Woman Walking (seen from behind)*, c. 1930–32, charcoal on paper, 66 × 54 cm, Dorich House Museum

Front flap: *Head of a Young Chinese Woman*, c. 1930–31, charcoal on paper, 66 × 56 cm, Dorich House Museum

Frontispiece: Plate 1 *Javanese Woman, Johor Bahru*, 1935, oil on canvas, 89 × 48.3 cm, Abbott & Holder, London

CONTENTS

LIST OF ILLUSTRATIONS

FIGURES

PLATES

Plate 2 Female Nude Torso in Red c.1930–31
charcoal on paper, 66 × 56 cm
Dorich House Museum

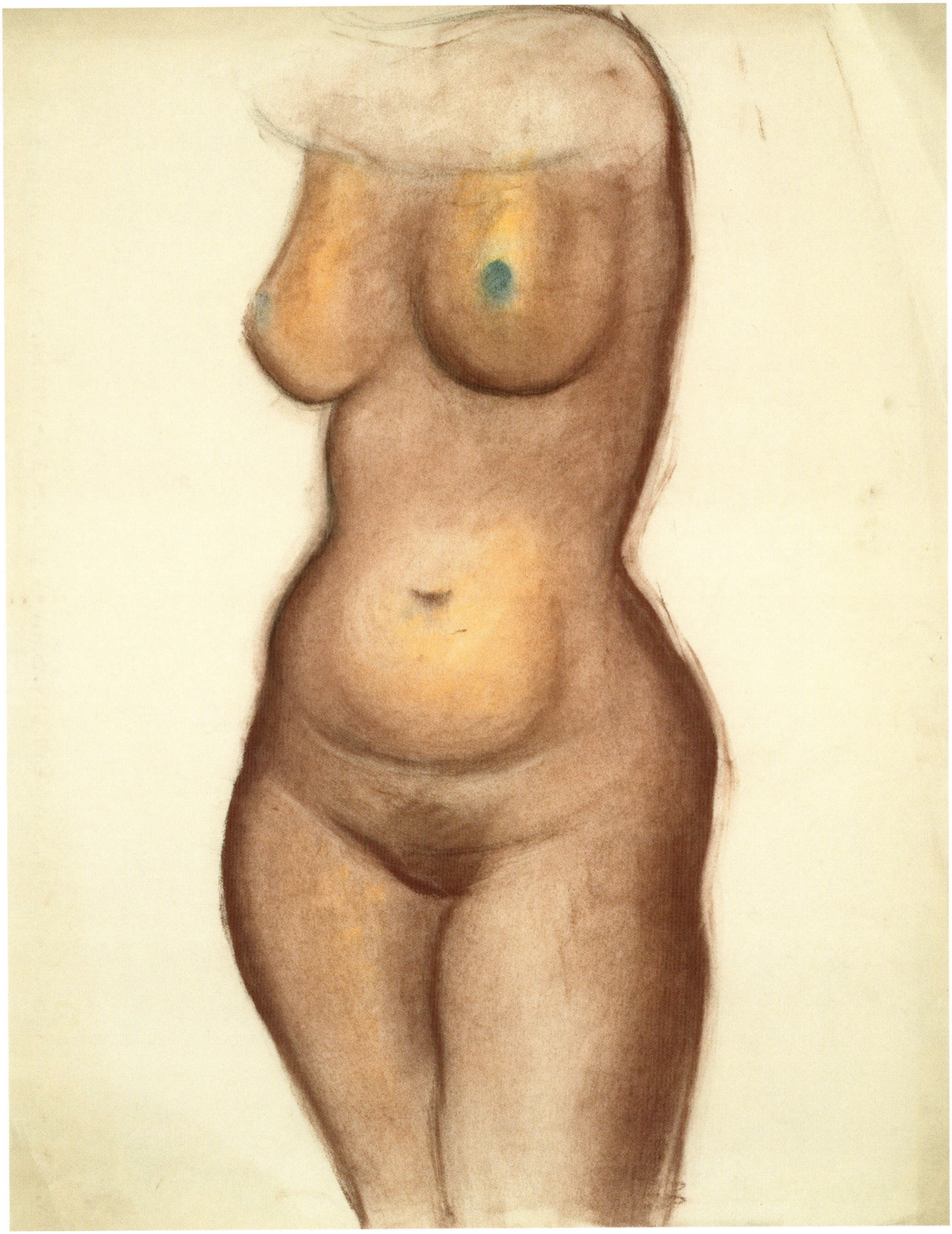

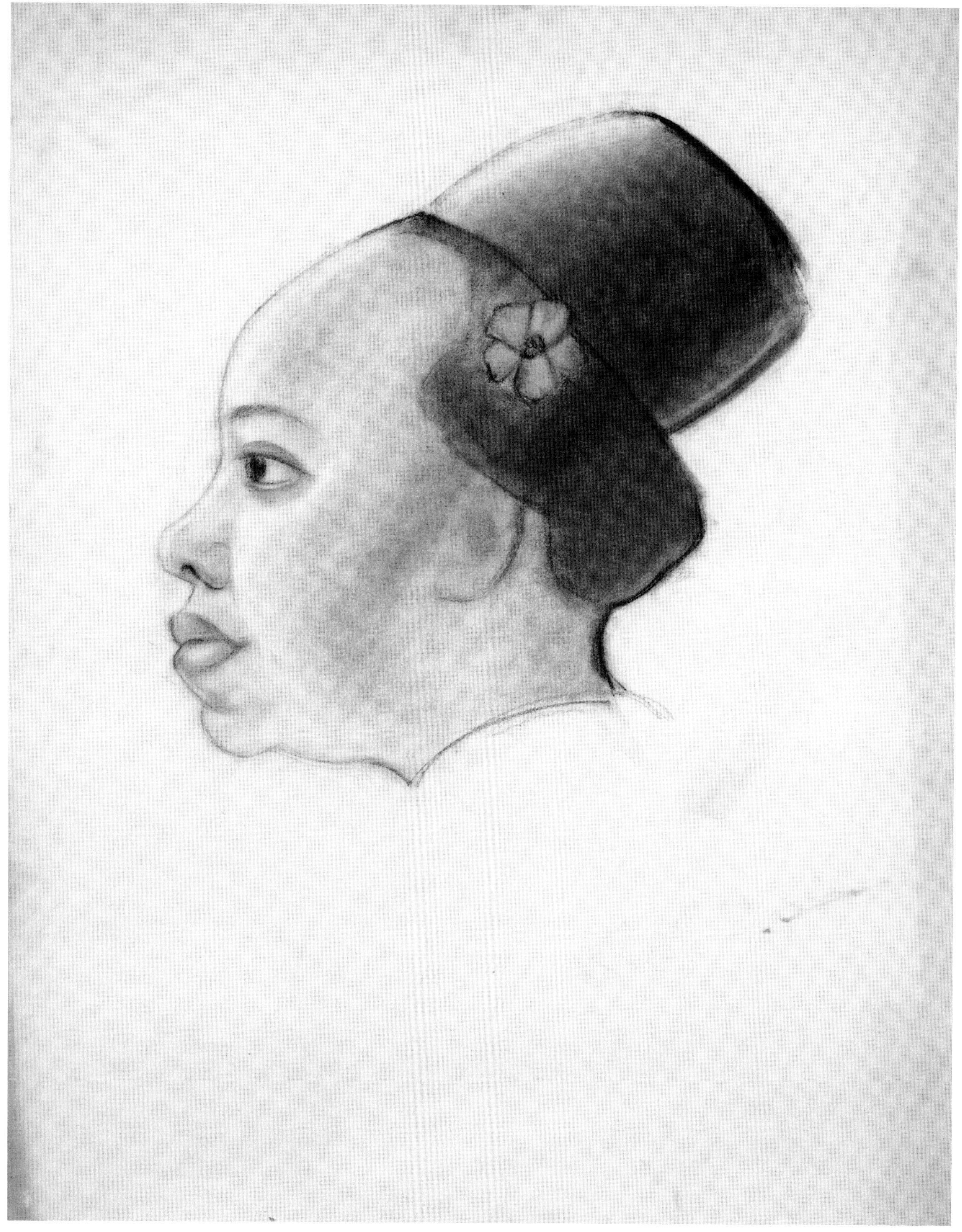

INTRODUCTION

Jonathan Black and Fran Lloyd

Throughout her distinguished career, the qualities of subtlety and strength were consistently ascribed to the sculpture and drawings of Dora Gordine.[1] Her surviving drawings – a strikingly eclectic group of 280 in the collection of Dorich House Museum, Kingston University – can be divided into a number of categories: sketches of individuals sitting for portrait heads; more finished drawings of people from the indigenous cultures of Southeast Asia c. 1930–35 [Plate 3]; sketches of subjects of the then British Empire in Asia, i.e. Malaya and Sarawak (1930–35), and of the then Dutch East Indies – especially from the island of Bali c. 1934–35 [Plate 4]; finished drawings of individuals who visited Dorich House c. 1937–39 [Plate 7]; finished drawings of diplomats and military attachés belonging to various embassies of countries allied to Britain during the Second World War – often from the Middle or Far East [Plate 16]; preparatory studies for public commissions, usually figurative, c. 1936–63 [Plate 5], and numerous studies of student ballet dancers in a multiplicity of poses, c. 1945–early 1950s [Plate 6]. The collection also includes a rare Paris sketchbook c. 1927–28, presumably one of many, which provides a fascinating insight into Gordine's interests at the time [Fig. 1]. Alongside small charcoal drawings of her 'ethnic' heads such as *Guadeloupe Woman*, and nudes of both sexes, it includes measurements for sculptures, pen and ink sketches of stage sets, and furniture designs for her Paris studio interspersed with occasional shopping lists.[2] But Gordine was always passionately interested in the human face and form.[3] She never showed any interest in drawing other subjects such as animals or architecture.

Plate 3 Burmese Headman Wearing a Hat c.1931
charcoal on paper, 66 x 56 cm
Dorich House Museum

Fig. 1 Dora Gordine, Male Figures, c. 1928, Paris Sketchbook, Dorich House Museum

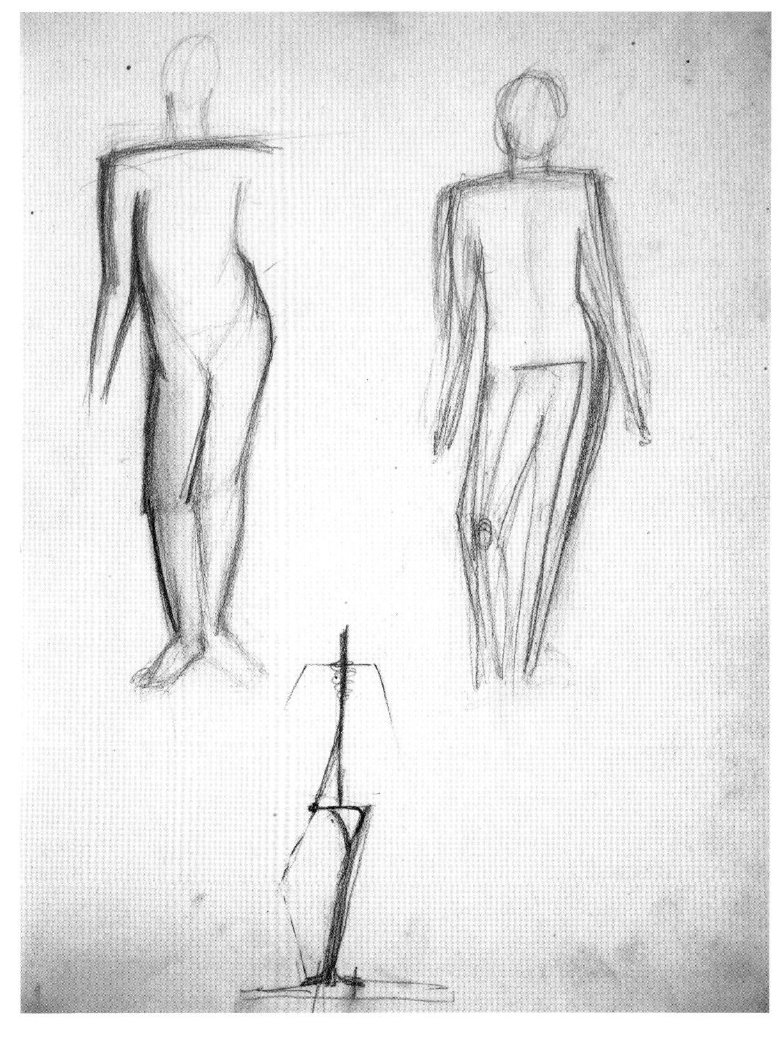

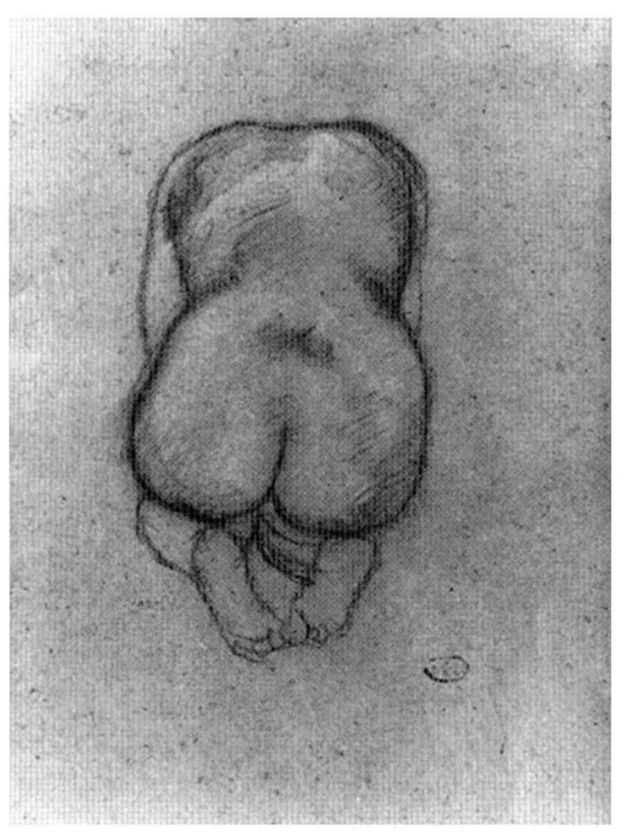

During her life, one of the very few of her artistic contemporaries Gordine admitted to admiring was Aristide Maillol (1861–1944), and her drawings do display some similarities with his – especially the treatment of the female nude [Figs. 2 and 3].[4] Gordine and Maillol shared a constant preoccupation with maintaining 'purity of line' and a rugged integrity of form in their art. In an interview she gave the *Straits Times of Singapore* in August 1930, for example, she stressed equally Maillol's importance as 'one of the greatest sculptors in Europe' and the need to record faithfully the 'excellent proportions and grace of line' evident in her indigenous sitters.[5]

She also expressed more guarded approval for the sculpture of Charles Despiau (1874–1946) and Joseph Bernard (1866–1933). However, her drawings invariably do not at all resemble theirs [Fig. 4].[6] Her treatment of the human form is far more emphatic and forceful than that of Despiau or Bernard; in this she pursued the impression of weight and substance that Maillol so often achieved. In similar fashion to Maillol she rarely sacrifices sensitivity or emotional richness for hefty presence. Though

above

Fig. 2 Aristide Maillol, Study of a Nude (Back), 1942, red chalk on paper, 30.4 × 20.3 cm, Private Collection, London

right

Fig. 3 Aristide Maillol, Female Nude (Dina Curled Up), 1939, red and white chalk on paper, 22.8 × 38.1 cm, Private Collection, France

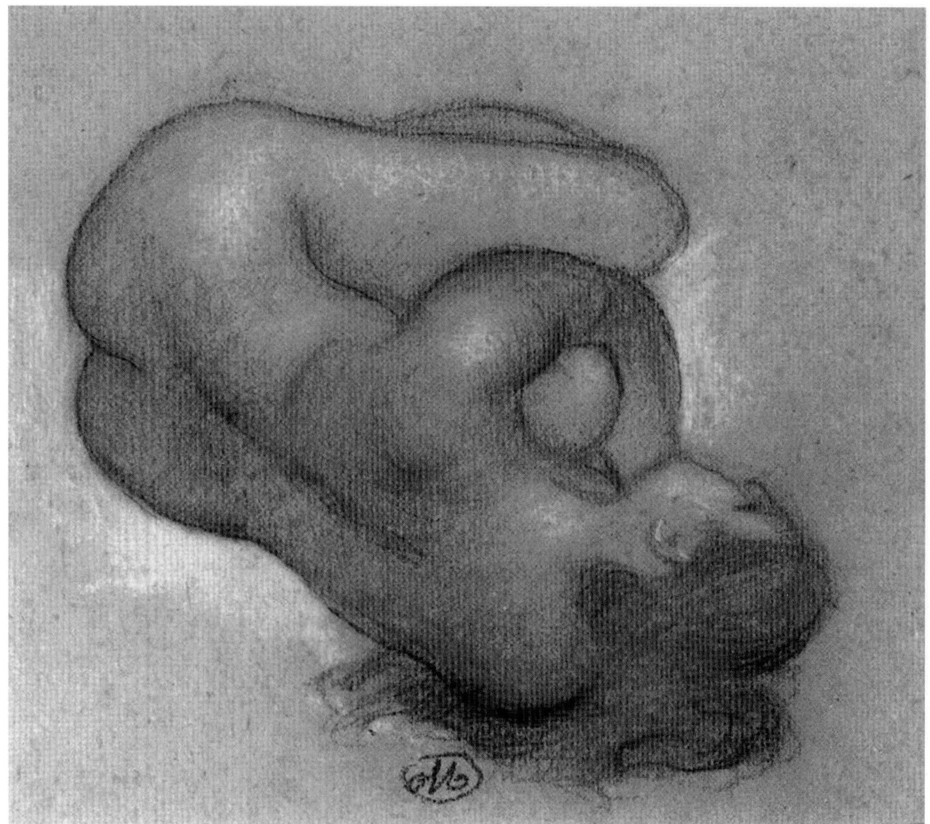

Plate 4 Bali Woman 1934–35
charcoal on paper, 66 × 65 cm
Dorich House Museum

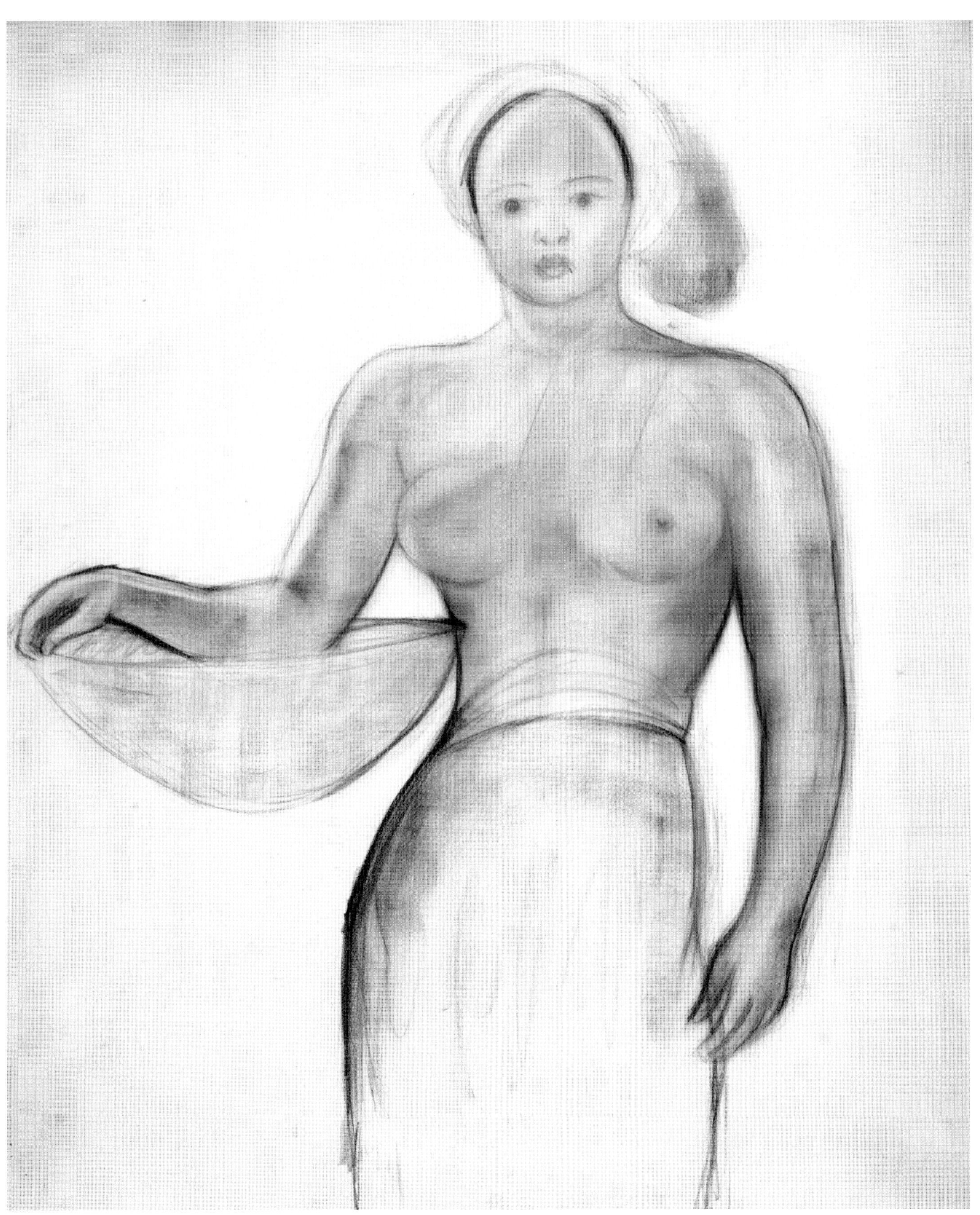

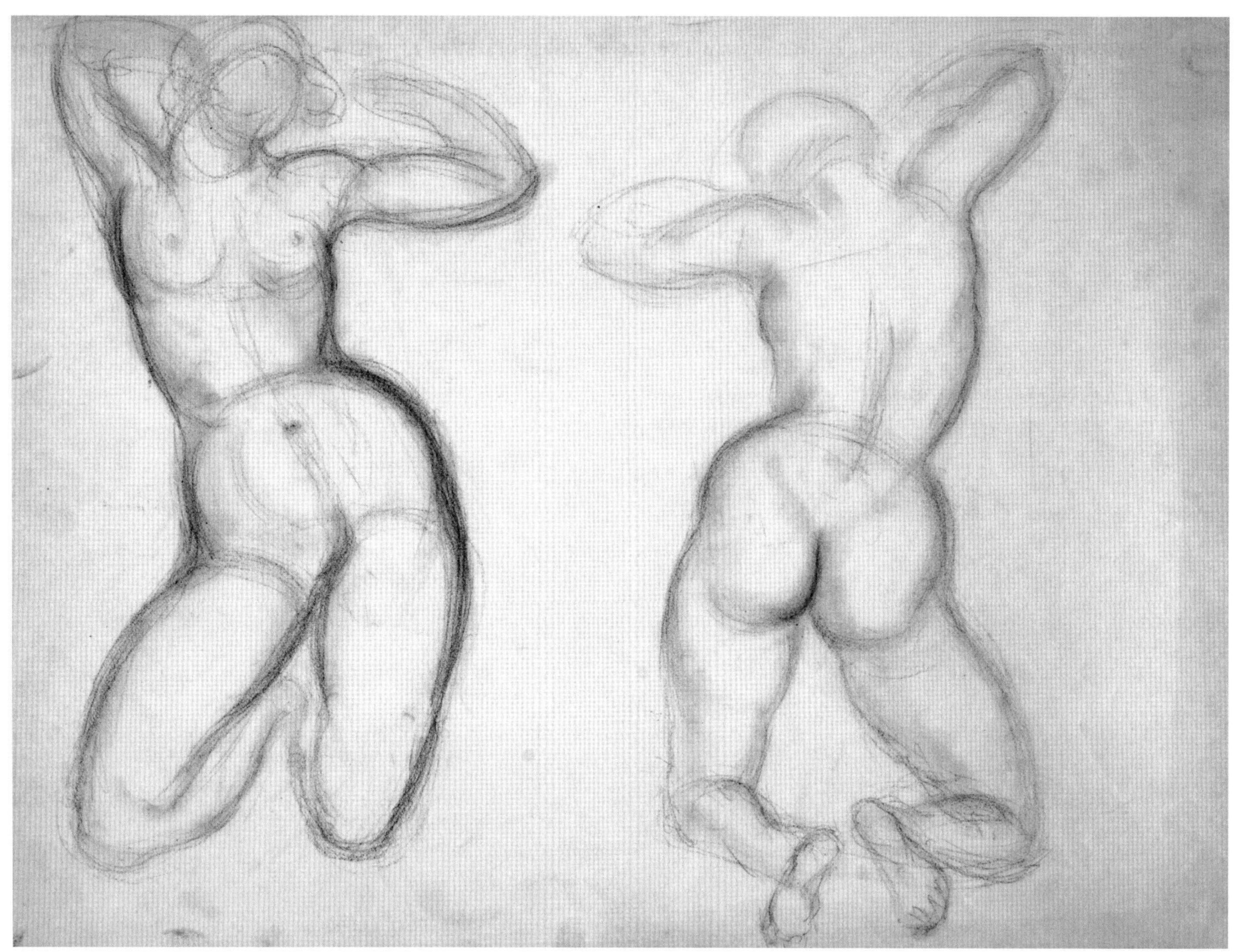

**Plate 5 Study for Crowning
Glory** 1946
charcoal on paper, 65 x 50 cm
Dorich House Museum

British critics, such as Frank Rutter and P.G. Konody, often likened her bronze portrait heads, especially of exotic, non-Western European sitters, to those produced by Jacob Epstein (1880–1959), her drawings do not remotely resemble his [Fig. 5].[7] Again, her emphasis is on power and presence while Epstein's line is more delicate, understated and even tentative.

Her drawings, especially those produced between the wars, have more in common with the approach to portraiture and the figure adopted by some of her German contemporaries – whom she may have encountered in Berlin in 1929 through Alfred Flechtheim – such as Käthe Kollwitz (1867–1945), Georg Kolbe (1877–1947) and Otto Dix (1891–1969) [Fig. 6]. Indeed, these three artists were all represented by Flechtheim during the 1920s, while he gave Gordine a solo exhibition at his Berlin and Düsseldorf galleries from September to October 1929.

Meanwhile, Gordine's drawings from the period, and after the Second World War, also readily invite comparison with work by a number of her British contemporaries, such as Frank Dobson (1886–1963) – himself strongly indebted to Maillol's sculpture from the mid-

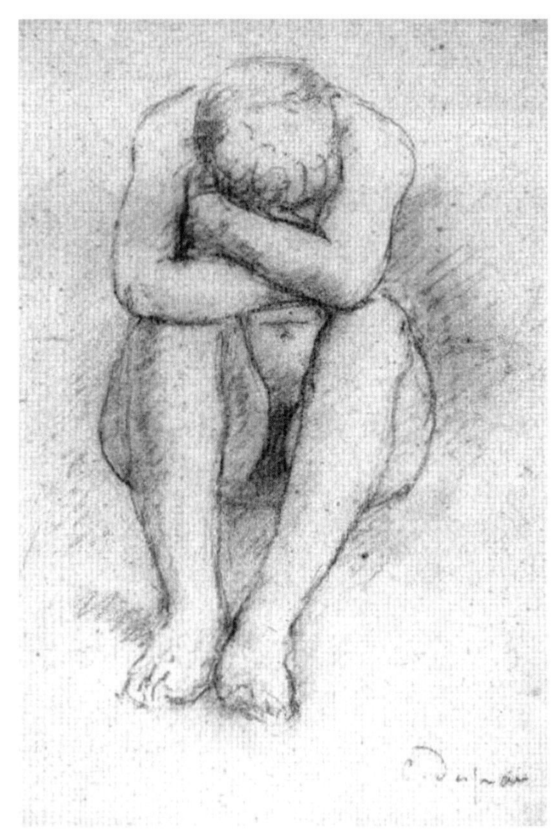

above
Fig. 4 Charles Despiau, *Seated Female Nude*, 1920s, pencil and red chalk on paper, 30.4 x 22.8 cm, Private Collection, France

left
Fig. 5 Jacob Epstein, *The Little Negress*, 1928, pencil on paper, 47.6 x 55.9 cm, Tate, London

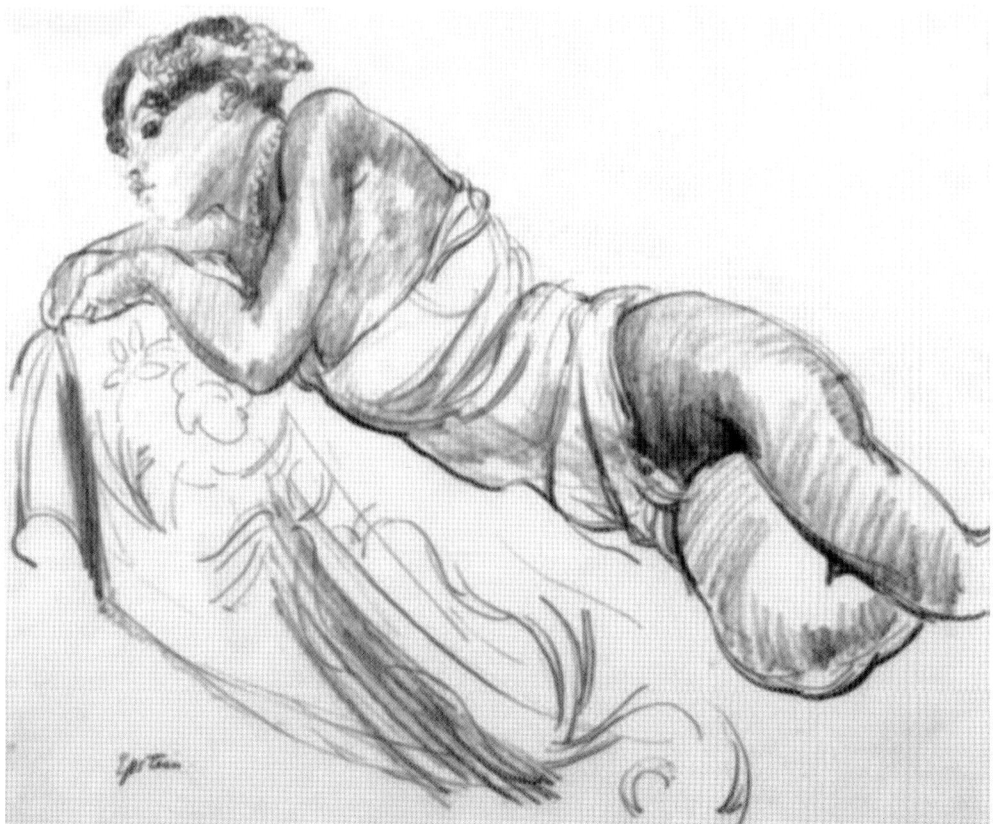

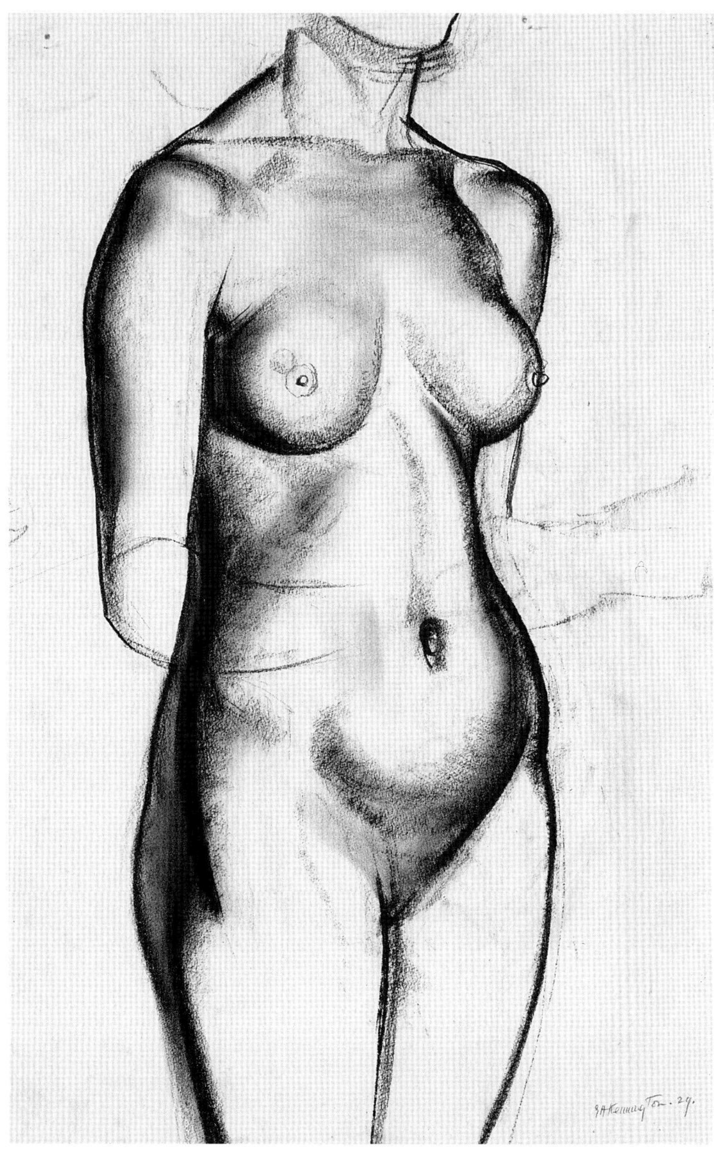

1920s onwards;[8] Eric Kennington (1888–1960) [Fig. 7],[9] Henry Moore (1898–1986) [Figs. 8 and 9][10] and Leon Underwood (1890–1975). Just like Gordine, they forcefully communicate a sense of bodily weight and muscular substance. The one occasion upon which she actually exhibited a body of drawings was in November 1938 at the Leicester Galleries in London.

Exhibits 1–21 (out of fifty-one) were drawings displayed in the Entrance Gallery and included studies of Balinese women (1–7 and 11–13, exhibited as *Beauties of Bali*), portraits of journalist Godfrey Winn [Plate 9], charity worker and champion of rights for the disabled Dame Georgiana Buller, art historian John Pope-Hennessy, child sitters Helen and Margaret Henderson, the former Sikh chief of police for Singapore Sardar Bahadur Sardar Mohan Singh, and a diplomat from the Persian/Iranian embassy (one of many contacts Gordine developed in the late 1930s with embassies from countries in the Middle East).

above

Fig. 7 Eric Kennington, Female Nude (Study for Unity), 1929, charcoal on paper, 53.8 x 34 cm, image courtesy of Osborne Samuel Ltd, London

right

Fig. 6 Otto Dix, Self Portrait, 1926, pencil and charcoal on paper, 30.5 x 22.9 cm, Private Collection, Berlin

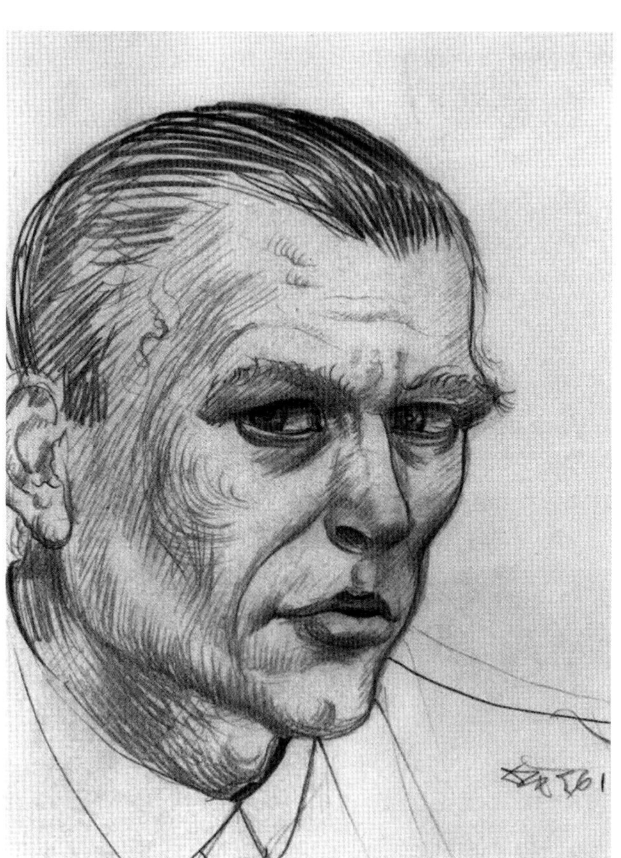

In the *Spectator*, Gordine's admirer, poet and critic Arthur Symons, commented enthusiastically:

> The drawings of Dora Gordine have these same sculptural qualities which many painters may envy and emulate – an absolute sureness of outline combined with a perception of depth and fullness, whether these are revealed in single heads or in complete or fragmentary figures. Far from being confined to preparatory sketches for sculpture, they are more in the nature of monochrome paintings with a precision of draughtsmanship and richness of shaded tones that give sensitive expression to every significant aspect of the subject … there are the heads, many of them portraits, and each one seems to breathe and to speak with a highly individual character.[11]

The drawings also certainly attracted the attention of a curator at the Victoria & Albert Museum who recommended to the museum's director, Sir Eric Maclagan, that he purchase at least one of her Bali drawings for a travelling display of the best in contemporary drawing.[12] Sir Eric promptly wrote to Gordine and paid her the considerable compliment in stating that her work, if purchased, would appear alongside examples already in the museum's collection by such significant figures as Jacob Epstein, Frank Dobson and Henry Moore.[13] It is pertinent to note that Gordine's work had already been recommended to Sir Eric by two of London's leading collector-philanthropists: Lord Ivor Churchill (1898–1956), a son of the 9th Duke of Marlborough, and Sir Mary Glyn (1859–1947), both of whom took a keen interest in contemporary art.[14]

In the end, though Gordine was keen to sell one of her drawings to the museum, the work selected by Sir Eric proved too large and too expensive. Evidently, she charged far more than any of her contemporaries and was not prepared to significantly reduce the asking price.[15]

Gordine produced the vast majority of her drawings as part of her sculptural process, whether for a portrait head, or a major public commission such as *Head of Sir Harry Vanderpant* (1937–38) [Plate 33] for the headquarters of the Royal Institute of British Architects, Portland Place, London; *Seated Baby (Miss Verena Dawnay)* (1937) [Plate 34] for Westminster City Council's new Maternity and Child Welfare Centre; the low-relief panel *Power* (1960) for the Administration Block, Esso Petroleum Refinery, Milford Haven, Pembrokeshire [Plates 36–38], or the imposing figure group *Mother and Child* (1962–63) for the entrance hall of the Royal Marsden Cancer Hospital, Sutton, Surrey [Plates 40–42]. In many cases, if she felt the sitter had an interesting face, Gordine would draw them for her own amusement. This was often combined with an unfulfilled expectation that they would then ask her to

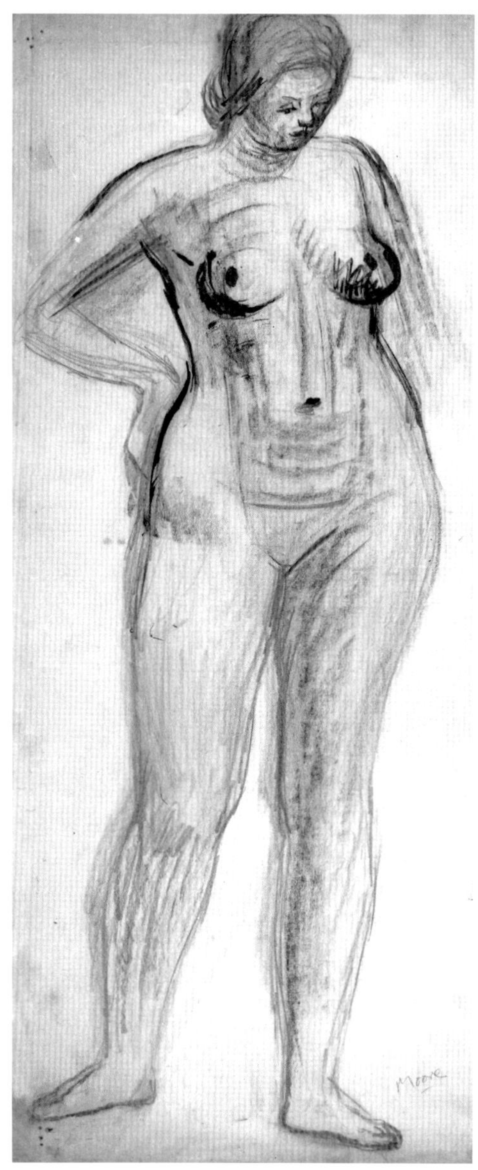

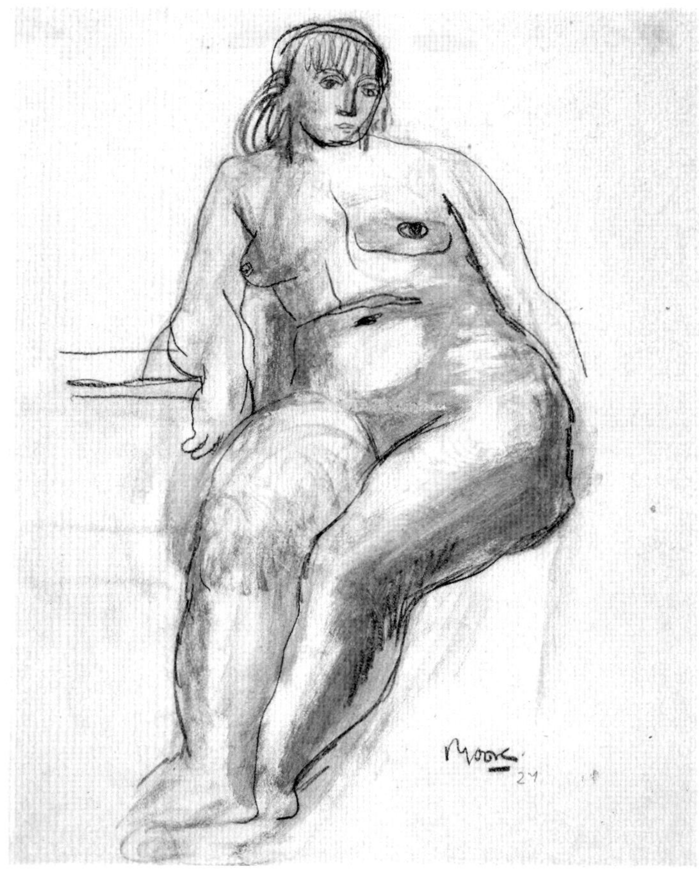

above

Fig. 8 Henry Moore, *Standing Female Nude*, 1927, chalk, pencil, and pen and ink on paper, 55.9 x 22.2 cm, image courtesy of the Henry Moore Foundation Archive

above right

Fig. 9 Henry Moore, *Seated Female Nude*, 1927, pastel, chalk and wash on paper, 42.5 x 34.1 cm, photo: Michel Muller, image courtesy of the Henry Moore Foundation Archive

produce a portrait head in bronze, i.e. with regard to drawings of *Godfrey Winn* in 1938, *Freya Stark* in 1939 [Plate 10], Chinese military attaché Colonel Huang in 1944 [Plate 15] and Professor Charles Storey, an authority on Arab literature, in the early '60s [Plates 20 and 21].

Most notably, as the following essays show, for Gordine the act of drawing was an intense and intimate one. Working with a range of sitters and models, the process of drawing was both a crucial means of becoming acquainted with her diverse subjects and of embodying their physical and emotional vitality [Plate 2]. Her drawings are material traces of the richness of these encounters over a period of almost fifty years. They also embody the evident pleasure that Gordine associated with the physical act of drawing.

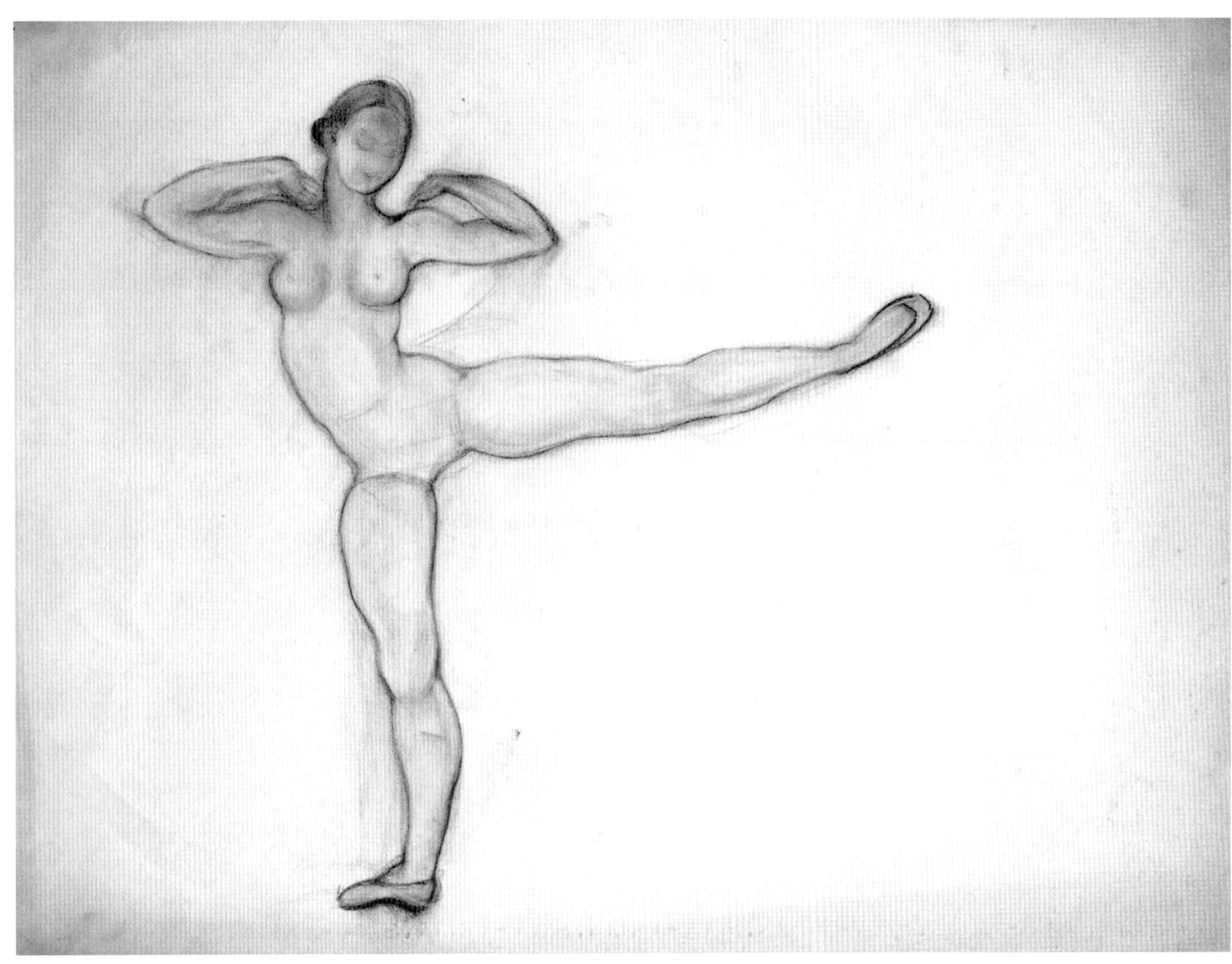

Plate 6 Study of a Ballet
Dancer c.1954–55
charcoal on paper, 64 x 66 cm
Dorich House Museum

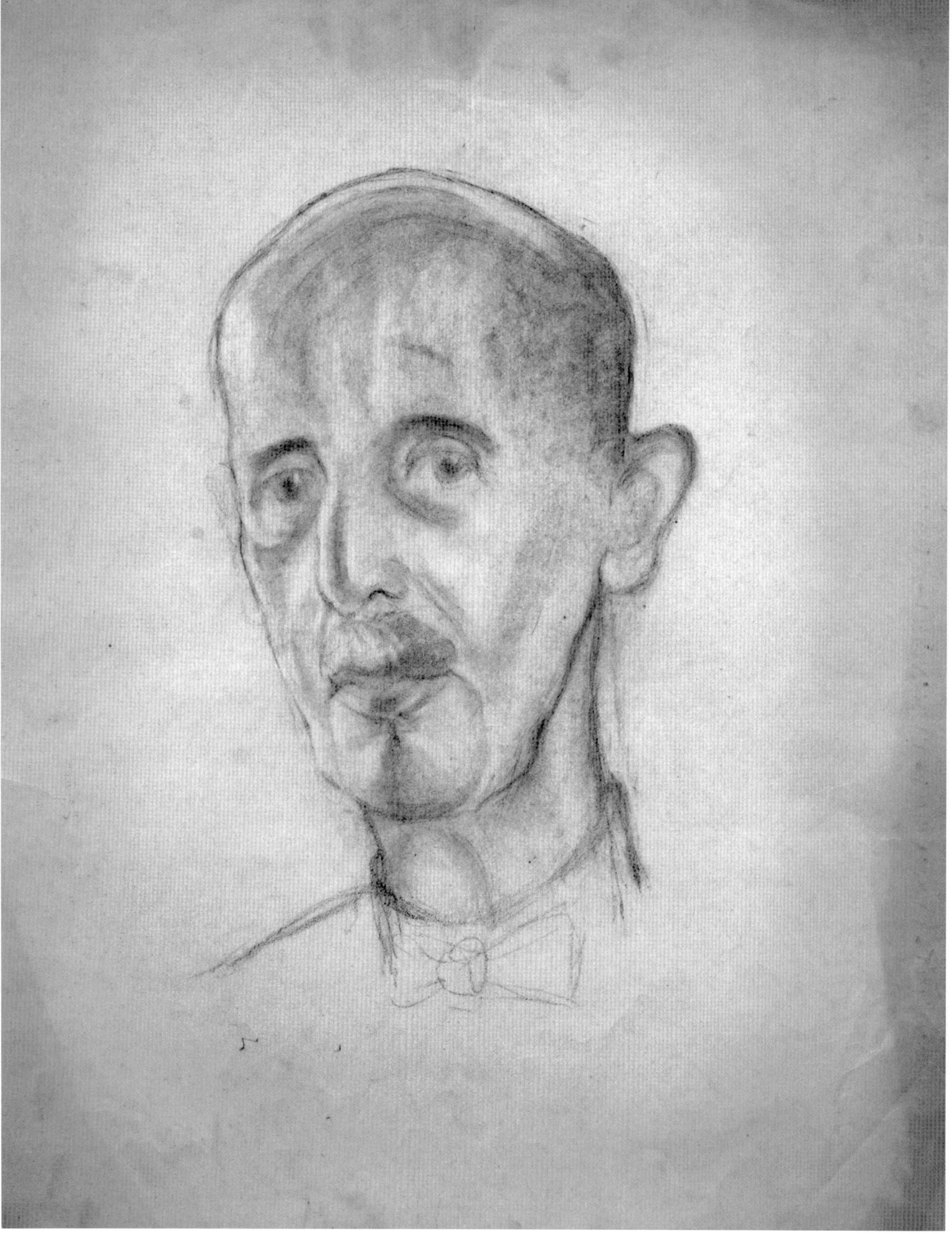

PORTRAITS OF AN AGE
c.1930s–60s

Jonathan Black

Many of the portraits Gordine produced in bronze and charcoal, once she had established herself at Dorich House, were of individuals who dominated the world of British high culture between the wars – prominent critics, writers, art historians, museum directors and curators, philanthropists and major art collectors.[1] They tended to be politically moderate, progressive in their social attitudes, and concerned with the plight of refugees from Nazi Germany or from war-torn China. Some could be found on the fringes of the world of the Bloomsbury Group and could be characterised as belonging to the mildly left-wing ranks of 'Our Age' as later defined by Lord Annan – a quintessential exemplar of the 'great and good' at the very apex of 'Establishment' Britain.[2] Upper-middle class, if male probably educated at either Oxford or Cambridge, comfortably off financially rather than being very wealthy, they gave themselves to public works and invariably sat on committees promoting an array of worthy causes en vogue at the time. These included widening access to fine art for the population at large, improving standards of maternity care, helping Jewish refugees (after Hitler's rise to power) gain access to British universities and support for the cause of the embattled Spanish Republic (1936–39).[3]

Whether through chance or design, Gordine chose a good moment to establish herself on Kingston Vale, SW15. The economy throughout the UK was devastated by the ramifications of the Wall Street Crash of October 1929. However, by early 1934, certain areas in England, particularly the home counties and the south east, were experiencing a marked economic revival.[4] The London art world, which had been in the doldrums for the best part of four years, now began to show signs of life again. Speaking very generally, there was just more money available for art commissions and purchases, and Gordine benefitted from this development. She also proved highly adept in making the most of contacts within the upper reaches of the British artistic, theatrical and literary

Plate 7 Dugald Sutherland MacColl 1937
charcoal on paper, 65 × 53 cm
Dorich House Museum

worlds that she had already established in London – partly as a consequence of two well-received solo exhibitions held at the prestigious Leicester Galleries, Leicester Square, in October 1928 and July 1933. Even before the construction of Dorich house was completed in October 1936, she sought out key individuals whom she wished first to draw and then portray in bronze. These bronzes would form the heart of her last pre-war solo exhibition, held at the Leicester Galleries in November 1938. Such was the réclame of these people that bronze portrait heads of them on display would be bound to attract widespread critical attention and press publicity. Gordine was not proven wrong in this assumption.[5] In fact she was extremely good at handling the press and was far more attuned to the need for 'public relations' in maintaining a career than the majority of her artistic contemporaries.[6]

PREWAR 1936–39

Dugald Sutherland MacColl (1859–1948)

Gordine had been introduced to the British Impressionist painter, art critic, curator, art historian, watercolourist and poet early in the autumn of 1937 by the director of Christie's auction house, Sir Alec Martin.[7] MacColl [Plate 7] had been educated at University College London and Lincoln College, Oxford. In 1903 he helped found the National Art Collections Fund and promoted the careers of likeminded artists such as Philip Wilson Steer, James McBey, Camille Pissarro and Muirhead Bone. Between 1906 and 1911 he was keeper of the Tate Gallery's British Collection and from 1911 to 1924, keeper of the Wallace Collection. He was a trustee of the Tate Gallery of British Art (1917–27) and a member of the Royal Fine Arts Commission (1925–29). Between the wars he was art critic first for the *Saturday Review* (1921–30) and then for the *Weekend Review* (1930–40).[8] MacColl was very taken with Gordine and willingly agreed to write the preface to Gordine's November 1938 exhibition catalogue.[9] For her part, Gordine was delighted by his agreement, writing to him in April 1938: 'Thank you so much, I appreciate it deeply. I am going to miss you and your scintillating talks and sparkling looks on Sunday mornings! … I am so excited to know you are going to write the preface for my exhibition.'[10]

For his portrait head, MacColl agreed at Gordine's insistence to shave off the moustache he had worn since his early 20s; he was then aged 79 years old. This tidbit of intriguing information was quickly leaked to the *Daily Telegraph* and duly appeared in his column in the newspaper.[11] It would appear that Gordine was very much relying on MacColl to remind many of his important and influential friends, such as Sir Robert Witt (1872–1952), then chairman of the National Arts Collections Fund; Lord Crawford (1871–1940), then chairman of the Royal Fine Arts Commission; Sir Kenneth Clark, then director of the National Gallery, and painter Philip Wilson Steer (1860–1942), to attend the private view of her 1938 Leicester Galleries exhibition.[12]

In December 1938, MacColl warmly supported a plan to donate a cast of Gordine's life-sized bronze *Walking Male Torso* to the University of London for display within the main lift hall of the recently opened Senate House Library on Malet Street, Bloomsbury.[13] The proposal, which was readily adopted by the university, was also backed by the library's architect, Charles Holden, Sir Eric Maclagen, Sir William Reid Dick (sculptor to King George VI) and H.S. Goodhart-Rendel (then president of the Royal Institute of British Architects).[14]

George Eumorfopoulos (1937–38)

Eumorfopoulos (1863–1939) [Plate 8], or 'Eumo' as she invariably referred to him, played a key role in launching Gordine's artistic career in the UK. He was probably introduced to her c. 1927 by Ernest Franklin, father of Geoffrey who was the business partner of her close friend David Gourlay. He, in turn, had been Gordine's joint entrée, along with his future wife, Janet Vaughan, to the influential world of Bloomsbury.[15] Gourlay and Vaughan were both familiar with Leonard and Virginia Woolf, and Vanessa and Clive Bell, as well as Duncan Grant and David 'Bunny' Garnett. Franklin senior and 'Eumo' both shared a passion for ancient oriental *objets d'art.* By the mid 1920s Eumorfopoulos had assembled a world-renowned collection of ancient Chinese and Persian ceramics and sculpture. Indeed, in 1921 he was founder member and first president of the Oriental Ceramics Society.

The fact he wrote an introduction to the catalogue of Gordine's first exhibition, at the Leicester Galleries in October 1928, was quickly noted by many critics and conferred upon her immediate respectability. Endorsement from 'Eumo' virtually guaranteed press attention and conveyed the strong impression that she was an artist of considerable talent. In its positive review of Gordine's exhibition, for example, the *Daily Express* commented: 'Mr George Eumorfopoulos, the great connoisseur, whose collections of Oriental sculpture and pottery is the finest in the world, introduces this young sculpturess to England. This is a great compliment for a beginner.'[16] He was later described as 'Gordine's first patron in England.'[17]

Eumorfopoulos was even better known by the time of the 1938 exhibition, when Gordine's cast of the head was first displayed. In 1934 he sold for much less than half of its market value two thirds of his immense collection of Han, Tang and Sung ceramics, sculpture and paintings to the British Museum and the Victoria & Albert Museum.[18] He also collected sculpture and drawings by contemporary British artists such as Epstein, Dobson, Hepworth and Skeaping. Examples of these and the bronze head of him by Gordine were on display in his studio for a 'weekend at home', at 7 Chelsea Embankment, that he hosted in January 1939 to raise money for 'the Chinese Universities Relief Fund of International Student Services for the assistance of Chinese students rendered destitute by the war in China'.[19] The bronze head of 'Eumo' was first exhibited in Gordine's solo show of November 1938 when it was widely singled out for critical praise.[20]

Godfrey Winn (1908–71)

Homosexual actor, author and journalist, Winn [Plate 9] achieved widespread public recognition during the 1930s. He started his acting career in 1924 with Sir Edward Marsh as his patron. Marsh introduced him to a circle of gay writers including J.R. Ackerely, Noel Coward and Beverley Nichols. In 1928 Winn met Somerset Maugham and, for a short period, they were lovers. The same year Winn published his first novel *Dreams Fade*. By the time he sat for a charcoal portrait by Gordine, in September 1938, Winn was one of Fleet Street's highest paid journalists and gossip columnists – first for the *Daily Mirror* (1936–38) and then for the *Sunday Express* (1938–42). After work as a war correspondent (1939–40), Winn served as an ordinary seaman for the remainder of the Second World War.

The noted historian David Kynaston has recently commented on how popular Winn was, especially among female readers, in the late 1940s and early 1950s.[21] Alan Bennett has also recalled that he enjoyed reading Winn in the 1950s, and continues to think of him as 'one of a breed of popular writers [including] Beverley Nichols, Phyllis Bentley and J.B. Priestley … Who impinged on our lives as more celebrated literary practitioners, Virginia Woolf, say, or Evelyn Waugh, never did.'[22]

In his 1967 autobiography, Winn mentioned being encouraged during the 1930s by Lord Beaverbrook, owner of the *Daily Express*, to focus on:

the kind of subjects that lit my own imagination. Such a visit I paid soon afterwards to the studio of Dora Gordine, the sculptress, who lived in a red-brick house with an unfruitful air from the outside on Kingston Hill. The atmosphere was transformed the moment one was inside and entered the embracing studio with one wall of windows looking out onto Richmond Park. I spent an enchanted afternoon and at the end of my tour I found myself again and again looking to the head of a Chinese girl [*Kwan Nin – Chinese Goddess of Mercy*, c. 1930–31] raised on a plinth; an exquisite creation, her eyes gazing downwards, with veiled lashes, as though she

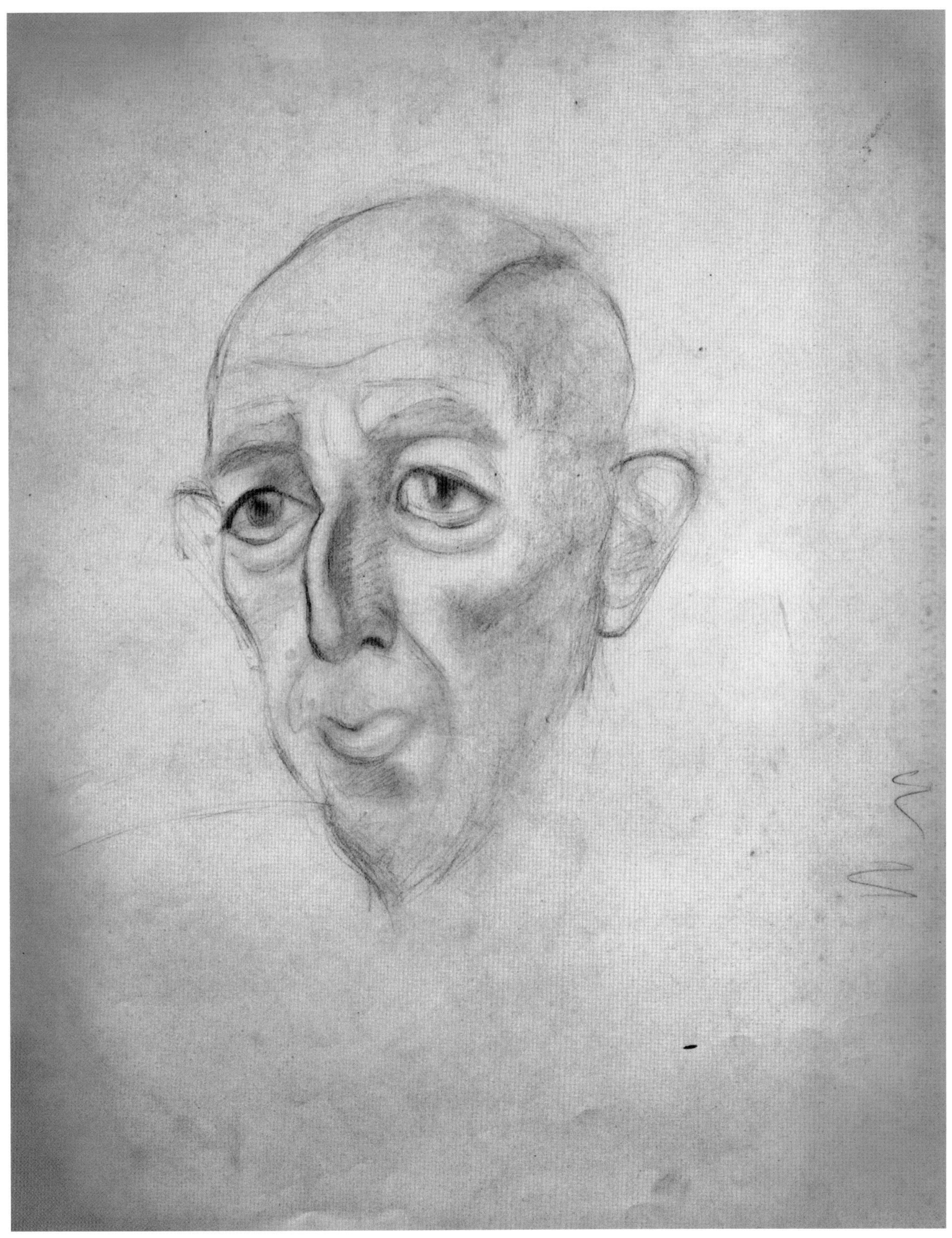

were dreaming away eternity. After a silence of contemplation, I turned to my hostess beside me and exclaimed "If I could afford an example of your work that is the head that I would love to possess!" "I'm afraid that is only a cast, the original has gone to a museum," its creator replied.[23]

Winn could have already met Gordine, or at least heard of her, through Noel Coward who had briefly encountered the artist in Singapore in 1935 when they sat near each other at a dinner held at Government House.[24] Gordine may possibly have met him again in the company of Maugham as she and her husband Richard went to stay at the Villa Mauresque on the French Riviera in January 1952 – during a period when Winn frequently visited the writer.[25]

Freya Stark (1893–1993)

A pioneering travel writer and intrepid explorer whom Gordine drew in February 1939, Stark [Plate 10] first came to public attention in June 1933 when the Royal Geographical Society awarded her the Back Memorial Prize for travelling widely alone though Persia and Iraq during 1930–31.[26] In 1934 she became even better known when the Royal Asiatic Society awarded her the Burton Memorial Medal – the first time it had been given to a woman – and *In the Valley of the Assassins*, her best-selling account of exploring the Levant, was published. Two years later she also published an account of her 1934–35 trip to Yemen, *The Southern Gates of Arabia*. It was immediately hailed as a classic of travel writing and Stark was awarded the Mungo Park Medal for Exploration by the Royal Scottish Geographical Society in December 1936.[27]

Stark was first introduced to Gordine by Sir Sydney Cockerell, formerly director of the Fitzwilliam Museum, Cambridge. He had taken Stark around Gordine's exhibition at the Leicester Galleries in November 1938,[28] and soon afterwards, in early December 1938, Gordine met Stark and Cockerell at a weekend house party given by Lady Violet Leconfield at Petworth House in Sussex.[29] Leconfield would later be drawn in charcoal by the sculptor at some point during the early 1940s.

Only a fortnight after the gathering at Petworth House, Stark came to dinner at Dorich.[30] She presumably enjoyed the experience as she soon called again, this time in the company of Cockerell and mutual friends cartoonist Osbert Lancaster and Stark's publisher Jock Murray.[31] At the time, Stark was in love with Murray but her feelings were not reciprocated.[32] Towards the end of February 1939 she sat to Gordine for the portrait in charcoal. The sculptor wrote soon after to Sir Sydney Cockerell: 'Freya Stark came [to Dorich House]; I made a drawing of her, I think quite good with [a] very highly strung expression …'[33]

It is a testament to Gordine's personal magnetism that she persuaded

Plate 9 Godfrey Winn 1938
charcoal on paper, 65 x 50 cm
Dorich House Museum

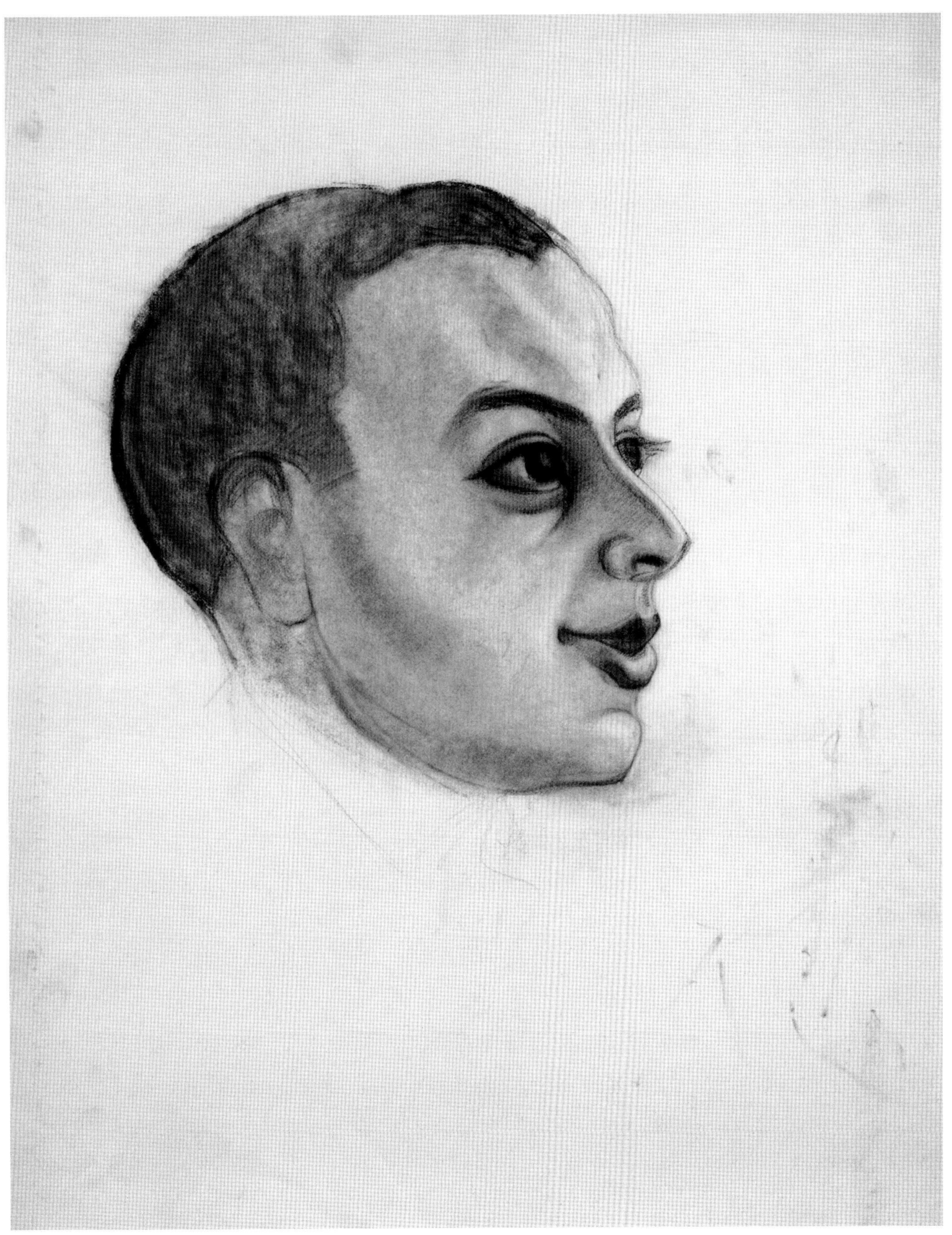

Stark to sit for her at all, as the writer was extremely self-conscious about her physical appearance. As a child she had a terrible accident in an Italian textile factory during which 'Half her scalp was ripped off, including her right ear; the right eyelid was pulled away and all the tissue around her temple exposed.'[34] For years after she endured a series of painful skin graft operations in an attempt to conceal the damage. Indeed, only the year before, she endured another session of cosmetic surgery to conceal 'the scars around her temple and eye.'[35] Her most recent biographer, Jane Fletcher Geniesse, has written that, throughout her adult life, Stark would 'cheerfully have had her body completely reconstructed if she could have done so, because she was acutely appreciative of beauty in others and felt its absence keenly in herself.'[36]

Collectively, these factors perhaps explain why Stark appears to be decidedly anxious and vulnerable in the portrait and why she declined to accept the drawing as a gift – and would not agree to Gordine's suggestion that she sit for a sculpted portrait head in bronze.

However, they did remain friendly for many years afterwards. They met several times during the Second World War in London when Stark was on leave from demanding duties for the British Colonial Office encouraging the formation of pro-British discussion groups in Egypt and Iraq.[37] She greatly admired the sculptor and her work, purchasing at least two of Gordine's statuettes of ballet dancers during the 1940s, and, in her third volume of autobiography published in 1953, wrote towards the end of the 1930s:

> I had begun to think … I might be one of those women who hate other women and are only easy with men: but now I realised what I dislike is the arrogance of the unforgiving woman, neither one thing nor the other. The lovely and the brilliant, or good, of my own sex: Celia Johnson; Biddy Carlisle; Phyllis Balfour; Vita Nicholson; Virginia Woolf; Dora Gordine and many others I met and admired and easily love – great people, all moving like queens in their own atmosphere …[38]

WARTIME 1939–45

For a short period in the early 1930s (1930–32) Richard Hare had worked in the Foreign Office. At the outbreak of the Second World War he rejoined the service and then was transferred to the Ministry of Information as personal assistant to the comptroller of overseas publicity. Gordine found herself having to cope with the running of Dorich House alone as her servants gave notice to join the war

Plate 10 Freya Stark 1939
charcoal on paper, 65 x 50.5 cm
Dorich House Museum

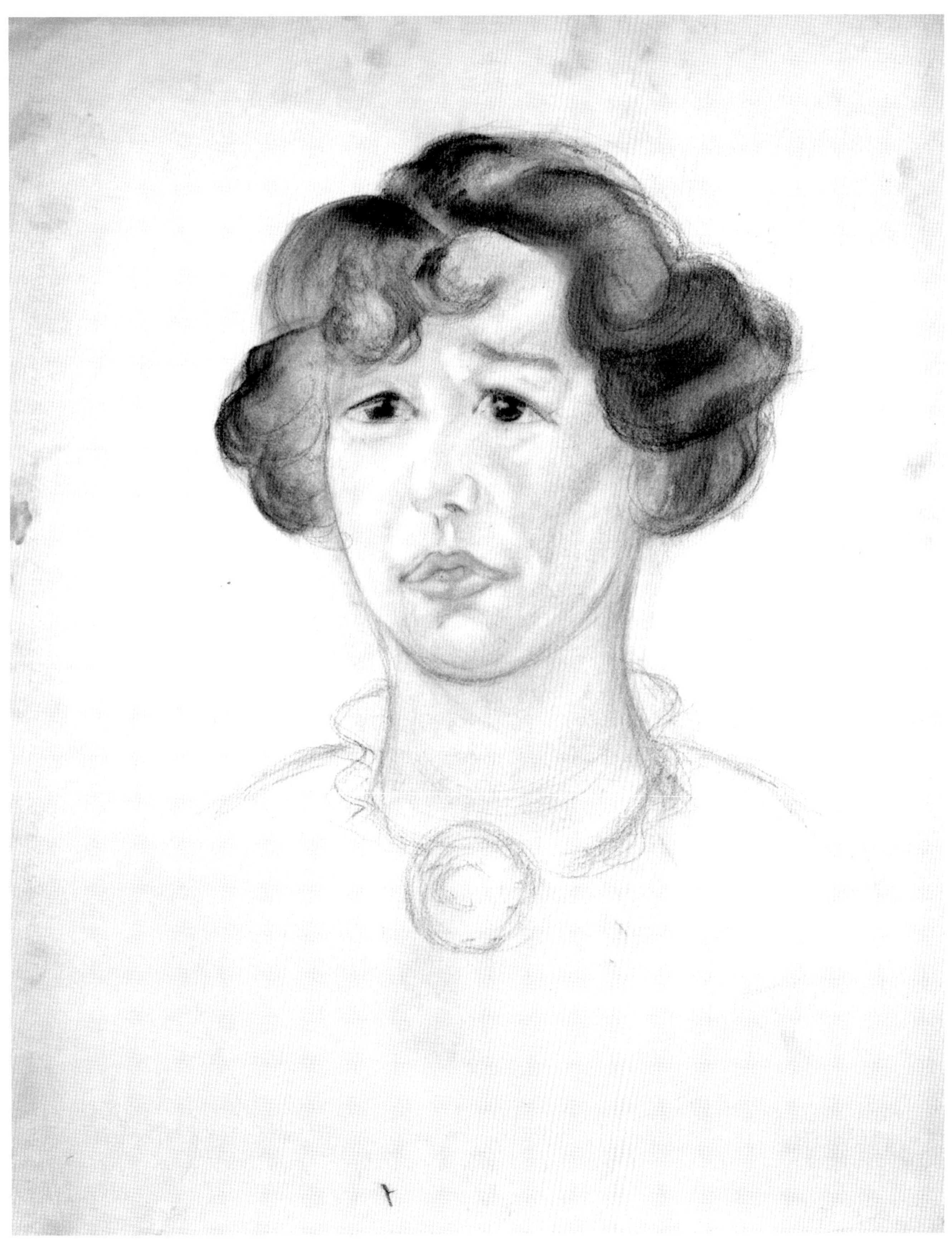

effort.[39] She looked to her support network of friends and pre-war admirers to sustain herself and made a number of unsuccessful attempts to find employment as an official war artist with the War Artists Advisory Committee at the Ministry of Information. In March 1942 Richard was promoted to work as a senior specialist advisor to the new and increasingly important Anglo-Soviet Relations Division.[40] In June 1941, Germany had invaded the Soviet Union, which until then had been her ally. By the end of the year it became clear that the Soviets were not about to collapse and, indeed, were now shouldering the main burden of the war effort against Germany. With his new position Richard acquired much greater status, providing him with access to an official car and a rare, officially sanctioned, petrol ration.[41] He moved in ever more elevated diplomatic and military circles, especially after his promotion to deputy director of the division in 1944, and brought a number of high-ranking individuals such as military attachés from embassies allied to Britain to visit Dorich House, admire Gordine's sculpture and be tempted to sit to her for charcoal portraits.

Violet, Lady Leconfield (1892–1956)

Born Violet Rawson, she married Charles Henry Wyndham, 3rd Baron Leconfield (1872–1952) in 1911. Charles was later appointed lord lieutenant of Sussex 1917–49. Between the wars Violet [Plate 11] was a leading patron of the arts and friend of Augustus John and the sculptor Kathleen Scott, née Bruce, who later became Lady Kennet through marriage to ennobled Liberal politician Wayland Young. She was a patron to both the Royal Geographical Society, where she met and befriended Freya Stark, and the Royal Asiatic Society and frequently attended their meetings.[42] During the 1930s Lady Leconfield was also a pillar of the Anglo-French Art and Travel Society and a keen fund raiser for the Sussex Hospital for Women and Children.[43]

It is possible that Lady Mary Glyn introduced Gordine to Lady Leconfield during the autumn of 1938. She was present at a luncheon party given by Lady Glyn in November 1938, which was also attended by Gordine and Sir Eric Maclagan.[44] Gordine and her husband stayed with the Leconfields at a weekend party held at Petworth House early in December 1938. It was during this party, as has been mentioned previously, that Gordine met and befriended Freya Stark and Sir Sydney Cockerell.[45]

Lady Leconfield attended many of the lectures Gordine gave for the Royal Asiatic Society between 1940 and 1944, such as the one on Indian sculpture in June 1944 when proceedings were temporarily interrupted by a V-1 'Flying Bomb' noisily passing over the lecture theatre.[46] Towards the end of the war she allowed Gordine to produce a cast of her right hand with a highly burnished gold-coloured patina. This was exhibited in Gordine's October 1945 solo show at the

Plate 11 Violet, Lady Leconfield c.1940–42

charcoal on paper, 65 x 55 cm

Dorich House Museum

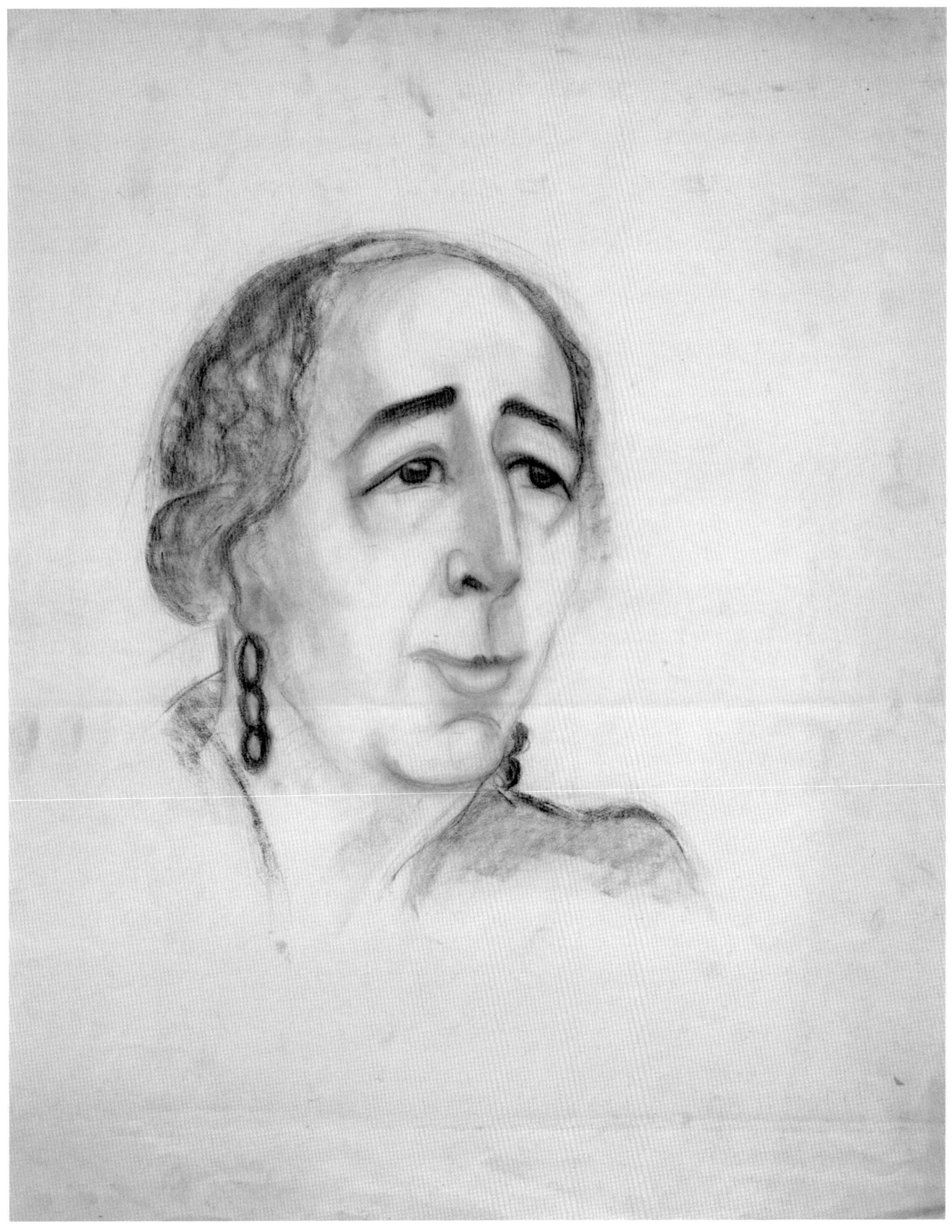

Leicester Galleries. Lady Violet, however, did not attend the private view for this exhibition, as she suffered from increasingly protracted spells of debilitating illness. Gordine did not see her so regularly and, indeed, expressed concern to Sir Sydney Cockerell that Lady Leconfield would not be able to mobilise her friends to come to the Leicester Galleries exhibition in 1945.[47] Gordine's charcoal portrait effectively presents Lady Leconfield as a woman who, though not conventionally attractive, possessed considerable charm and a powerfully convivial personality. Cockerell, who had come to know her well since their first meeting in 1937, believed she had a genuinely discerning artistic eye and was a more truly cultured person than better known and more attention-seeking high society hostesses such as Mrs Ronnie Greville, Lady Emerald Cunard and interior decorator Lady Sybil Colefax.[48]

Mrs Elsie Simon née Branton (1897–1976)

The sitter [Plate 12] was a neighbour of Gordine's who lived next door to Dorich House, in Robinwood Place, from c. 1937–47. She sat to Gordine for a portrait bust in 1943. In July of that year Gordine wrote vividly to Sir Sydney Cockerell suggesting the almost physical pleasure she derived from working with such an attractive body: 'I am working very hard. A great variety in work … [a] Voluptuous head and arms, back and breasts. A bust of a lady up to the waist – very exciting. Doing lots of drawings …'[49] Part of the reason for her palpable excitement and enjoyment was that she had produced little sculpture over the previous three years and had spent much of the spring of 1943 in bed recovering from an operation to remove her appendix that had taken an unusually long time to heal – this was an era pre-antibiotics and the NHS.

In 1924 Elsie Branton married newspaperman George Percival Simon (1893–1963). Five years later Simon was appointed advertising manager of the *Daily Telegraph*. By the beginning of 1939 he had risen to the position of general manager at the newspaper and confidant of its owner Lord Camrose.[50] Shortly after the outbreak of war he toured the United States with Elsie in an effort to improve Anglo-American relations and combat American isolationism. George Simon later remarked how much he had benefited during the tour from the presence of his wife, with her down to earth common sense and ability to mix well with Americans from all walks of life, holding diverse political opinions and usually lukewarm about the prospect of entering hostilities on the side of Britain. Apparently, Elsie proved a success even in Chicago – a centre of isolationist and anti-British feeling.[51] She impressed one journalist who interviewed her with the way in which she combined 'high-class London chic' in her dress and coiffeur with the depth of character associated with the fictional character 'Mrs Miniver' – a quietly heroic upper-middle class home counties housewife created by British

Plate 12 Mrs Elsie Simon
c.1943
charcoal on paper, 65 x 52 cm
Dorich House Museum

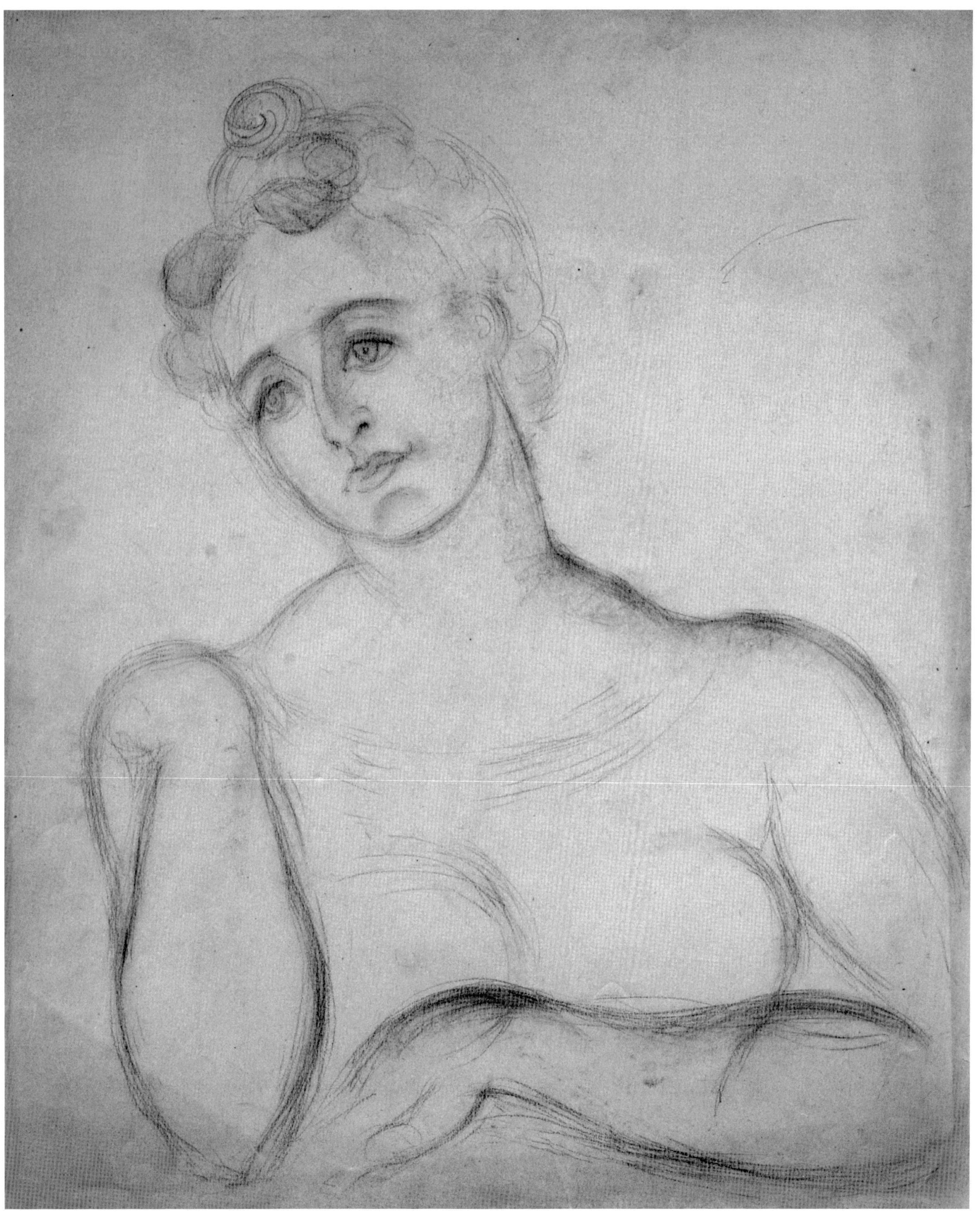

journalist Jan Struther (pen-name of Joyce Anstruther 1901–53) as a column for the *Times* in 1937, which was very popular with women of all backgrounds in the United States.[52]

Not long after sitting for the portrait bust, first exhibited at the Leicester Galleries in October 1945, both Elsie and her husband became closely involved in fund raising for the Rainer Foundation – a charity that sought to help young girls who 'got into trouble' or, in today's parlance, became 'gym-slip mothers'.[53] Hardly a fashionable cause for someone who, if glimpsed in the pages of the *Tatler*, might easily have been mistaken for an empty-headed socialite. However, though her husband worked for a deeply Conservative newspaper, both were extremely concerned about social problems afflicting the nation's youth. Indeed, in the general election of July 1945, Elsie voted for the Labour Party, convinced its policies would create a better future for the young.[54]

Major Lyudmilla Mikhailovna Pavlichenko (1916–74)

The formidable and deadly Major Pavlichenko [Plate 13] was a celebrated Red Army sniper who shot 309 'Fascists', i.e. Germans, while serving on the Eastern Front between August 1941 and June 1942.[55] Before the war she had been a history student at Kiev University. At the front she participated in the defence of Odessa and Sevastopol and was wounded four times before she was ordered back to Moscow and awarded the Order of Lenin for her sniping prowess. Indeed, she was one of the first and most effective students of the Red Army's Central Women's School for Snipers whose graduates, during the war, accounted for the deaths of over 12,000 Germans.[56]

In November 1942 she was in London to take part in a Soviet national day celebration organised by the Ministry of Information's Anglo-Soviet Relations Division, for whom Richard had been working since the beginning of the year. She then embarked on a tour of the south-east of England, visiting munitions factories to raise British civilian morale. Towards the end of the month she was in Kingston-upon-Thames to visit a factory that built Hawker Hurricane fighter aircraft.[57] Presumably, it was during this period that Major Pavlichenko visited Dorich House and sat to Gordine, who was also trying very hard at that time to obtain a position as an official war artist with the Ministry of Information.[58]

There is some intriguing evidence from a letter she later wrote to Sir Sydney Cockerell that Gordine did not enjoy the experience of meeting Pavlichenko, whom she found uncouth, surly and suspicious.[59]

Presumably, the ace sniper had been made aware of Gordine's White Russian connections, such as her brother Leopold fighting against the Bolsheviks in Estonia in 1919, and then there was the incongruity of her portraitist being married to Hon. Richard Hare, the son of an earl. Ironically, it has recently

Plate 13 Major Lyudmilla Mikhailovna Pavlichenko
1942
charcoal on paper, 49 x 39.5 cm
Private Collection, UK

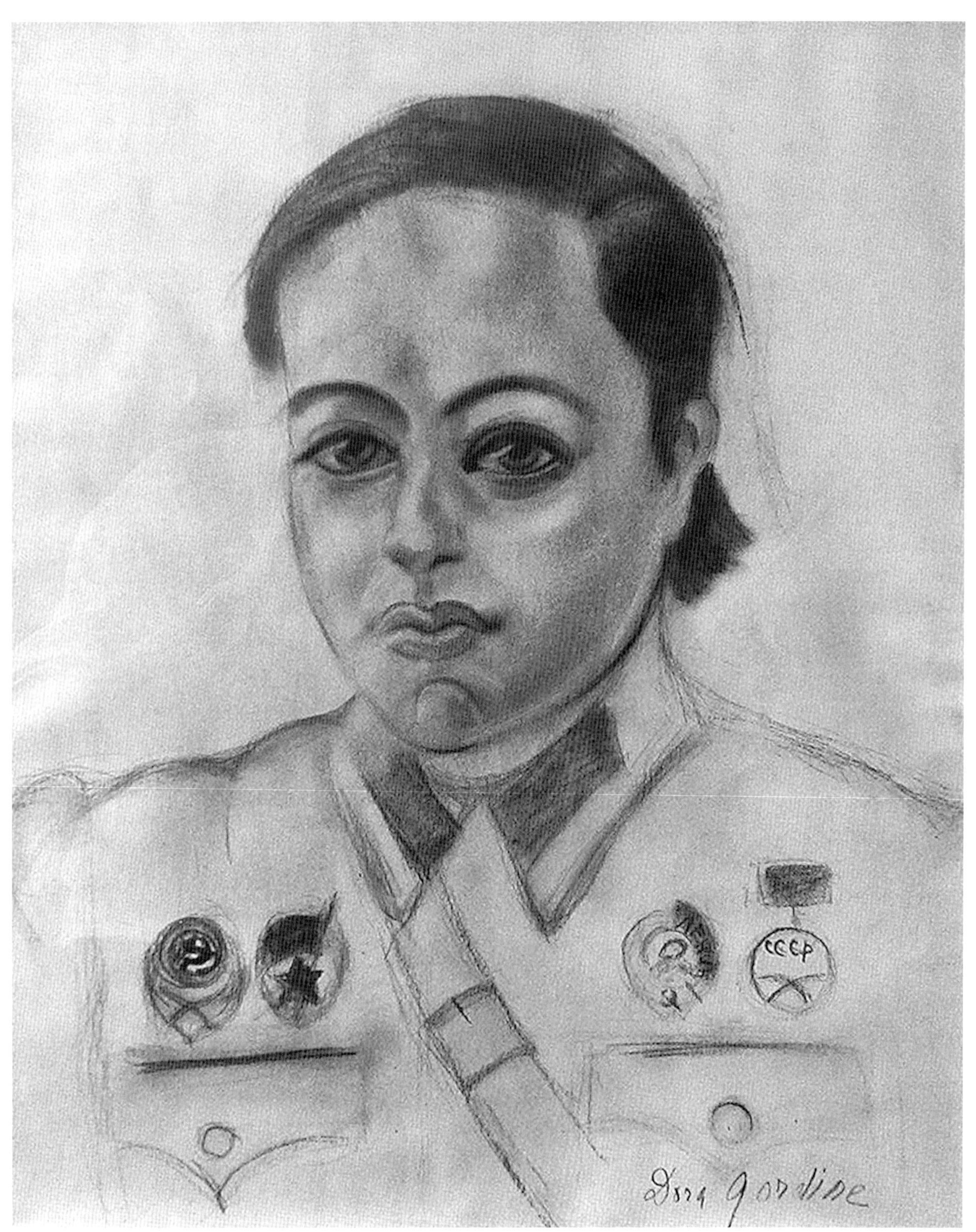
CCCP

emerged that Richard Hare's superior, and head of the Anglo-Soviet Relations Division from 1941 to 1945, Peter Smollett (real name Peter Smolka; 1912–80), was a Soviet spy feeding information straight to the NKVD.[60] In fact, the intelligence he was providing was so good that, for the first year that he was in charge of the division, his Soviet masters suspected him of being a double agent working for MI5. Smollett had joined the Ministry of Information in 1939 as a journalist and protégé of press magnate Lord Beaverbrook. Early in 1945 he even persuaded the publisher Jonathan Cape not to publish George Orwell's biting satire *Animal Farm* on the grounds that it slandered Stalin, a major British ally.[61]

Gordine must have been somewhat conflicted when drawing Pavlichenko, since she was a fanatical adherent of a creed and state that had destroyed the comfortable world of the Russian empire Gordine had known as a teenager before the First World War. Furthermore, in June 1940, the Soviet Union had brutally occupied Estonia, which Gordine called home from 1912 until 1928, when she left Tallinn to live full-time in Paris.[62] She probably did not know as she was drawing Pavlichenko that in June 1941 the Soviet secret police had arrested her elder sister Anna, still living in Tallinn, as a suspected 'bourgeois counter-revolutionary' and deported her, along with ten thousand other middle class Estonians (four hundred of whom were Jewish) to die from exposure in Siberian camps around Novisibirsk.[63] In a further twist to circumstances, by the time Pavlichenko sat to Gordine, Richard had translated the Russian text for the Anglo-Soviet treaty of May 1942 which, in a secret clause, recognised the legality of the flagrantly illegal Soviet occupation of the Baltic States since 1940. This ensured that the states, once they had been reoccupied by the Red Army in 1944, would remain under Soviet control until 1991; Russian troops did not in fact leave Estonia until August 1994.[64] Gordine, however, never appears to have shown the slightest interest in the fate of her relatives living in Tallinn: two months after the Germans captured that city, towards the end of August 1941, the SS shot her elder brother Nikolai – for being Jewish.[65]

Private L.G. Young

Towards the end of July 1943 this striking portrait of a Surrey Home Guard private [Plate 14], reminiscent of Marie Laurencin's stylised portraiture of the 1920s, was reproduced in the *Daily Telegraph*. Gordine described herself as a 'student of British types' and told the reporter that she had been trying to 'personify the special qualities of the Home Guard' in a series of charcoal drawings. She had apparently been drawn to Private L.G. Young because he immediately struck her as 'the real British type … with the dry smile she thinks characteristic of the English temperament. She has a theory that the plain living and hard working enforced by the war is leading to a better understanding of art by the greater

Plate 14 Private L.G. Young
1943
charcoal on paper, 66.5 x 53 cm
Dorich House Museum

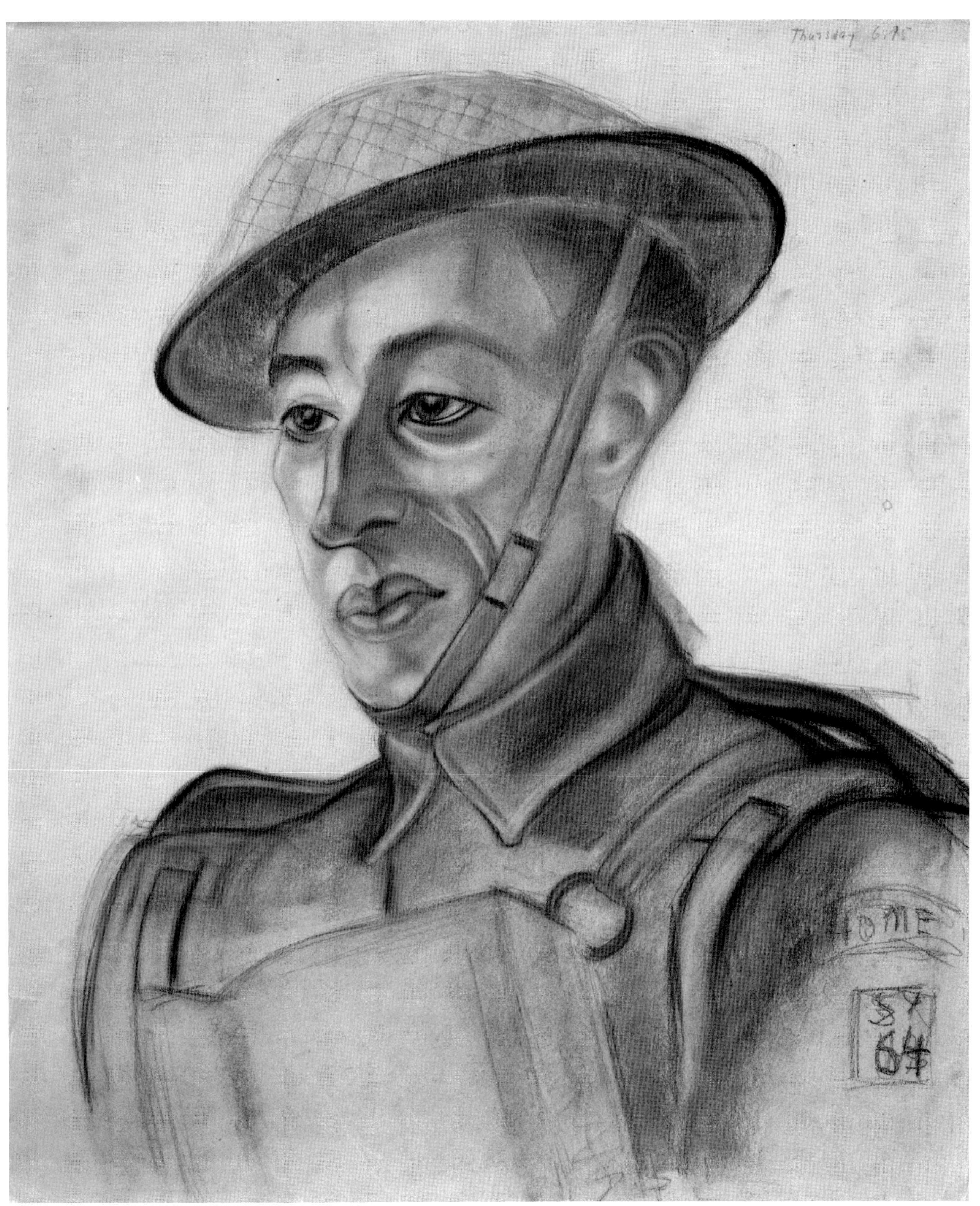
Thursday 6.15
HOME
SY
64
0$

public … Being of Russian extraction, Miss Gordine can bring to her study of British types a certain detachment.'[66]

The Home Guard had initially been established as the Local Defence Volunteers in May 1940 for men aged between seventeen and sixty-five not already conscripted into the armed services. Within a matter of weeks over one and a half million men had volunteered.[67] Private Young probably worked during the day in one of Kingston's many factories devoted to war production and then served in the Home Guard in the evenings. The success of the Home Guard project led to much reflection on the 'English', or the 'British', character. In 1941, George Orwell, who had previously served as a sergeant in the Kentish Town Home Guard, wrote of the common physical and behavioural characteristics of the men serving in it: small of stature with bad teeth and sunken cheeks – an indication of extremely inadequate pre-war nutrition – unimpressed by professional military hierarchy or 'swank' and utterly disdainful of their so-called 'betters', the politicians and generals. Yet he was convinced they would not succumb without a fight if the Germans invaded in 1940–41.[68]

As for Gordine, like so many of those comfortably off before the war, life on the Home Front compelled her into making contact with far more working class people than she ever had hitherto. Since March 1941 women aged between nineteen and forty had been obliged to register for some form of weekly war work with the Ministry of Labour.[69] It is not clear exactly what she did in London after her unsuccessful attempts to become an official war artist in 1942 but, by the spring of 1943, she was spending two days a week in the east end with the WVS (Women's Voluntary Service) helping local people who had been bombed out of their homes.[70] Whatever she was doing, she found it 'terribly interesting'.[71]

The article about Private Young in the *Daily Telegraph* also suggests she had adopted an Orwellian interpretation of the war's unforeseen beneficial effects, i.e. the privations, the rationing, the danger and, in her particular case, learning to do without servants and performing her own housework, were in the long run positive developments that served to strip away middle class snobbery and complacency.[72] What with fire-watching every night, her duties in the east end and the general difficulty of travelling around London in wartime, she found it a considerable struggle to make time for artistic work. Petrol rationing and the shortage of buses made travel to Dorich House from central London a daunting prospect.[73]

Colonel Huang

The irrepressible anglophile Colonel Huang [Plate 15], a devotee of P.G. Wodehouse, Dickens and the stories of Sherlock Holmes, was the Chinese Nationalist military attaché.[74] He was a habitué of so-called 'fork dinners'

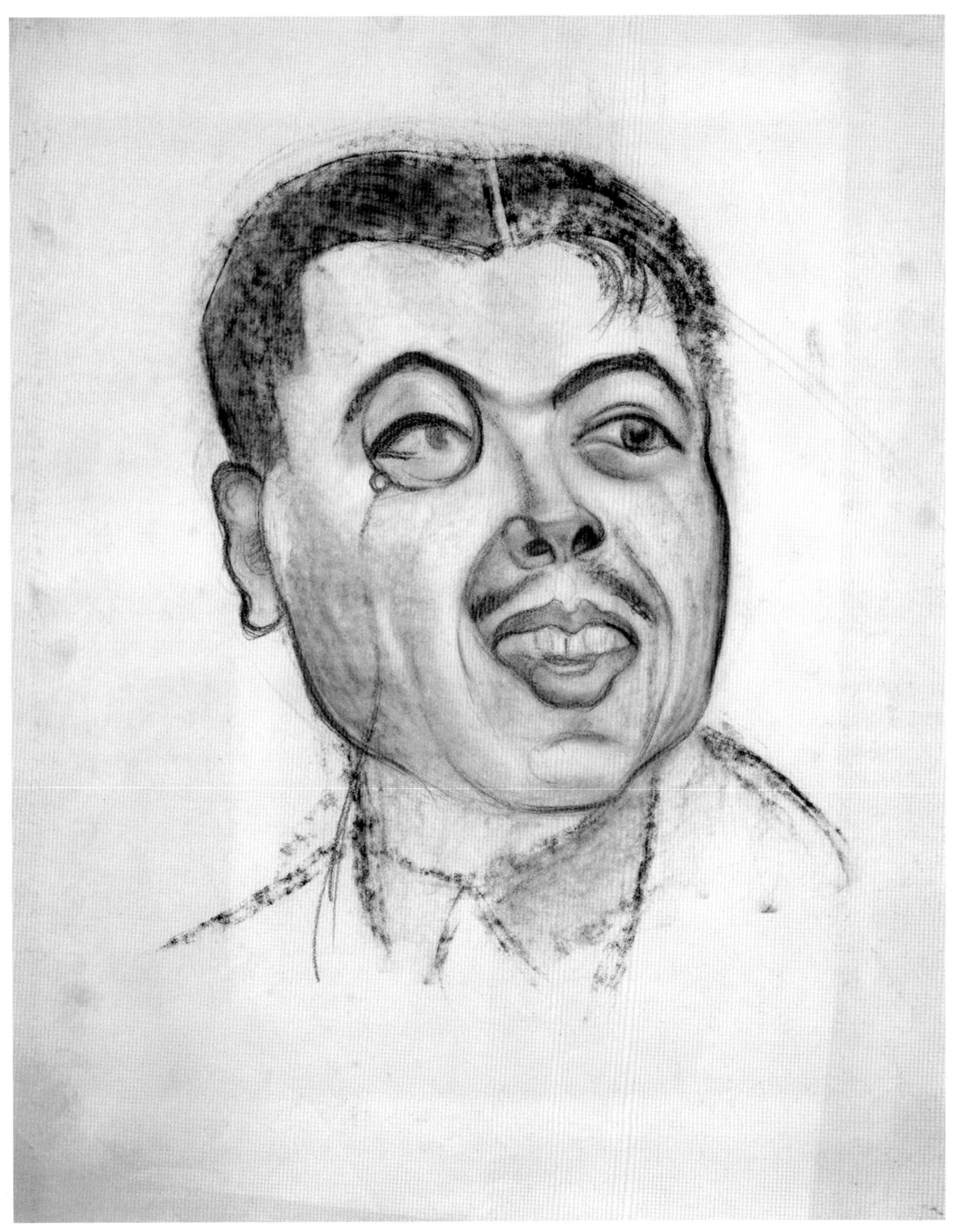

arranged by Lady Elsie Goold-Adams to promote greater international understanding among those counties allied to Britain and the USA.[75] Huang was, in fact, seen chatting animatedly with Gordine at a Goold-Adams 'fork dinner' held in September 1944.[76] Gordine could also have met the colonel through her brother-in-law, William, Earl of Listowel, who had close contacts with the Nationalist Chinese in London, and since 1938 had been president of the China Campaign Committee and, as a Labour peer in the House of Lords, a prominent supporter of Lady Cripps's 'British United Aid to China', which had the blessing of the Chinese Nationalist leader Generalissimo Chiang Kai-shek.[77] The colonel may well have attended a lecture she gave on Chinese sculpture at the Royal Asiatic Society in September 1944.

Around the time she drew Colonel Huang, Gordine was approached by a body with close links to the Chinese Nationalists, the Sun Yat-sen Memorial Committee, to produce a portrait plaque in low-relief of the father of the Chinese Nationalist Party and the first president of the Republic of China.[78] The relief was eventually unveiled in May 1946 just off Greys Inn Square by the Nationalist chargé d'affaires Mr C.K. Cze and with Colonel Huang in the audience.

There is more than a touch of caricature about Huang's portrait, and yet the end result is affectionate rather than displaying the forced emphasis on ugliness and distortion so often evident in the portraits produced by Otto Dix and George Grosz in the Weimar Germany of the 1920s [Fig. 6].

Dr Jaime Jaramillo Arango

His Excellency Dr Don Jaime Jaramillo Arango [Plate 16] was the Colombian ambassador to London from September 1940 to December 1945.[79] At the time Columbia was technically neutral in the Second World War but inclined strongly in favour of the Allied cause. Dr Arango, an admirer of Winston Churchill, was one of a stream of senior diplomats who visited Dorich House during the 1940s, including the ambassadors of Egypt (see below), Saudi Arabia, Iran, Indonesia, Estonia, Yugoslavia, Poland and Brazil. Gordine apparently first met him in the autumn of 1944 and quickly decided she wanted to draw and sculpt him.[80] As she later wrote to a female friend, although she was known for portrait heads of women, she always relished the opportunity to work on the more mature male sitters with 'interesting faces'.[81] Presumably, Dr Arango, who was known for being a witty and stimulating conversationalist, possessed one of these faces. Sittings for the bronze portrait head began in January 1945 and Gordine produced the charcoal drawing early in the process.[82]

The bronze head of Arango was included in Gordine's October–November 1945 solo exhibition at the Leicester Galleries. The sitter was present at the private view and declared himself delighted with the likeness Gordine had achieved.[83]

Plate 16 Dr Jaime Jaramillo
Arango 1945
charcoal on paper, 65 x 51 cm
Dorich House Museum

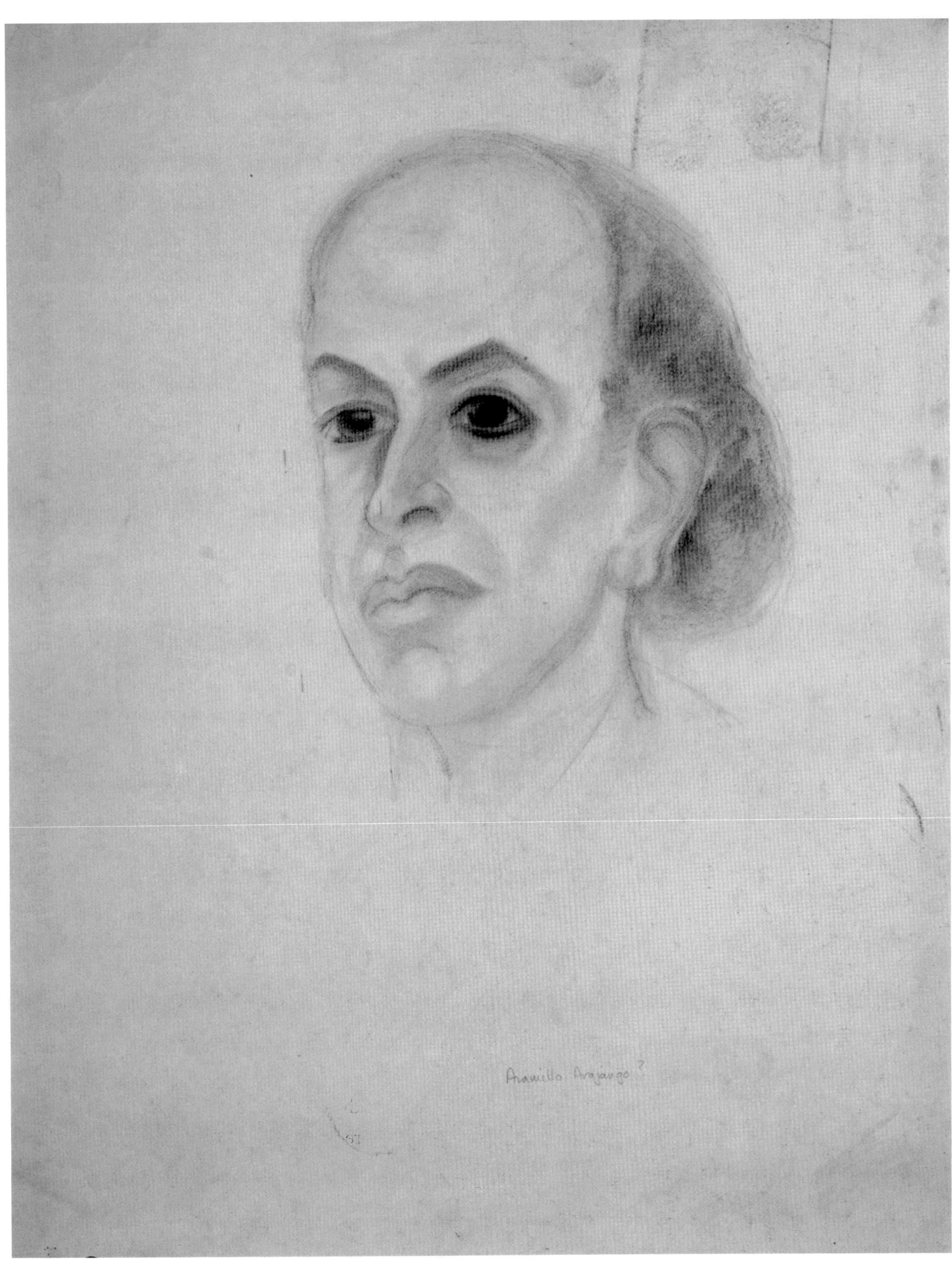

POSTWAR 1946–62

Abd-el-Fattah Amr Pasha

His Excellency Amr Pasha [Plates 17 and 18] was the Egyptian ambassador to London from August 1945 to August 1952. Previously, he had been legal advisor to the Egyptian embassy and found time to win the world amateur Squash Rackets Championship six times between 1931 and 1937.[84] He was a childhood friend of the future king of Egypt, Farouk II, and was widely regarded as pro-British before the Second World War and valued by the British Foreign Office for exercising a positive influence on his feckless, playboy monarch who reigned from 1936 to 1952.[85]

Gordine had already established good contacts with the Egyptian embassy before the war: during her time in British Malaya she befriended Sir Miles Lampson – future British high commissioner for Egypt (1933–46). During 1944–45 a frequent visitor to Dorich House was Moyine al-Arabi Bey, press attaché at the Egyptian embassy, who soon sat to Gordine for a portrait head commissioned as a wedding present by his future bride Gracie Weigall – daughter of famous 1920s Egyptologist and author of the popular book *A Short History of Ancient Egypt* (1934), Arthur Weigall (1881–1934).[86]

In December 1945 Amr Pasha presented the new Labour government with a demand from King Farouk that it fundamentally revise the Anglo-Egyptian treaty of 1936, leading to the removal of all British armed forces from the country – especially from the Suez Canal zone.[87] In July 1947, shortly after he finished sitting to Gordine for a bronze portrait head, Amr Pasha came to an agreement with Hugh Dalton, the Chancellor of the Exchequer, by which Dalton renounced control over the National Bank of Egypt.[88] However, despite this diplomatic success, Amr was widely regarded in Egypt as a tool of the British. Early in November 1948 his Cairo home was blown up 'by those who resent [his] indefatigable endeavours to set Anglo-Egyptian relations on a better footing.'[89]

Gordine's bronze portrait head of Amr featured in her exhibition at the Leicester Galleries in 1949. At the private view, another visitor to Dorich House, the Saudi-Arabian ambassador Sheikh Hafiz Wahba (1889–1967) was spotted 'looking intently at the head [of] a colleague from the Arab world … *Amr Pasha*, well known to the British public as the world's greatest squash rackets player. Everyone who knew him agreed that it is an excellent psychological likeness.'[90]

Early in 1951 King Farouk recalled Amr in protest at British obstruction concerning the future of the Suez Canal and appointed him as Foreign Minister. Unfortunately, however, this enraged the mob in Cairo and triggered a week of anti-British rioting in the capital.[91] In March 1952 Farouk sent Amr back to London as ambassador to London in a last effort to resolve the impasse over control of the

Plate 17 Abd-el-Fattah Amr
Pasha 1947
charcoal on paper, 65 x 52 cm
Dorich House Museum

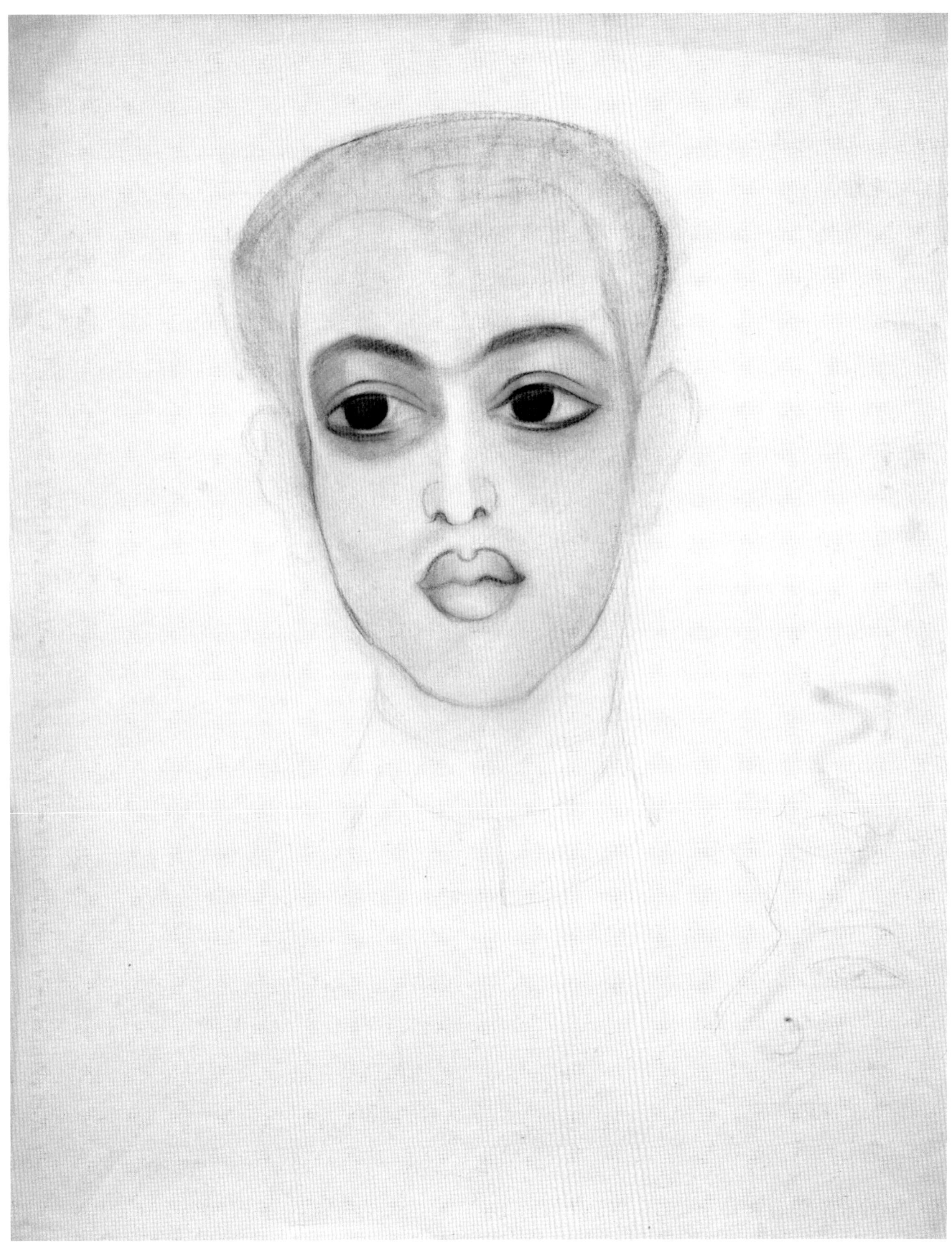

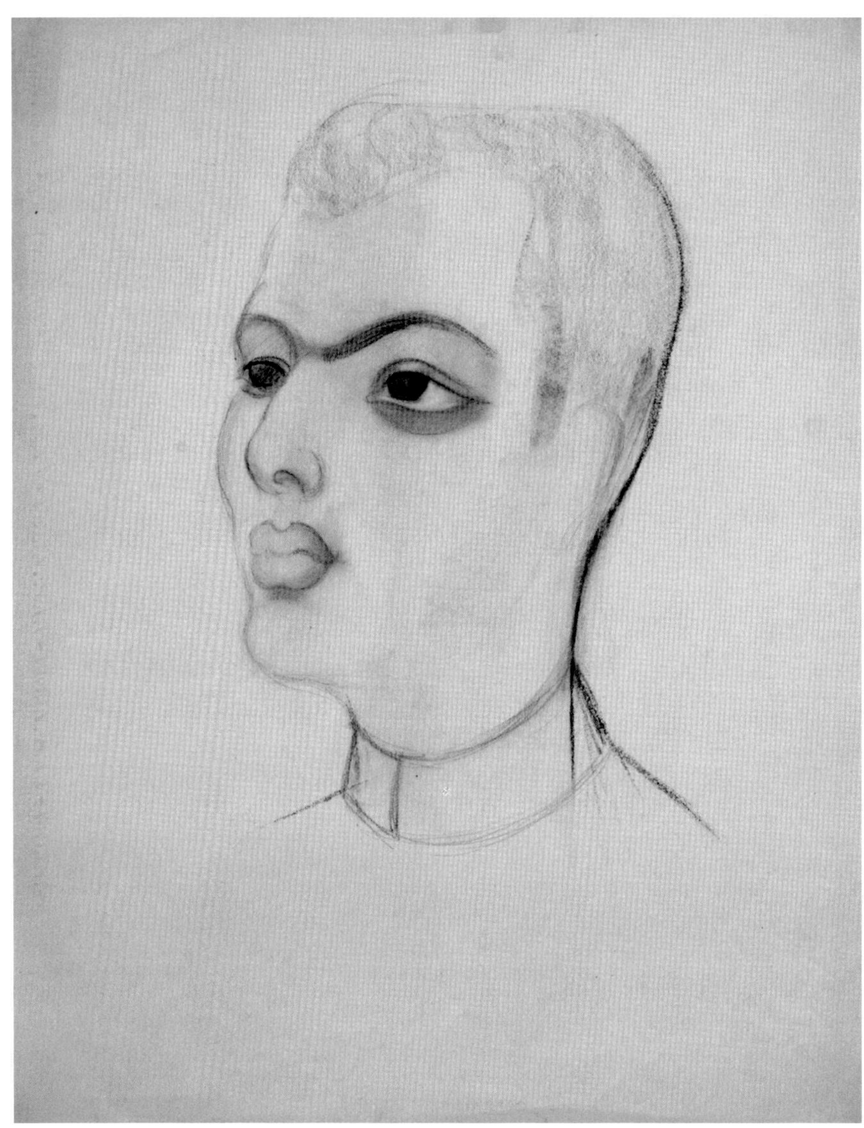

Plate 18 Abd-el-Fattah Amr
Pasha 1947
charcoal on paper, 65 x 52 cm
Dorich House Museum

Suez Canal. Four months later, however, King Farouk was overthrown by a group of young army officers led by Colonel Gamal Abdul Nasser in a sudden military coup. In August 1952 the new regime abolished the title of 'Pasha' and promptly recalled Amr to stand trial because he was regarded by Nasser as 'pro-British and, ipso facto, a hireling of the British Government.'[92] Unsurprisingly, Amr did not return to Cairo and certain death before a firing squad. He took refuge in London and eventually went to live in the south of France. As for Gordine and her husband, they felt sympathy for Amr while regarding his king as a buffoon whose overthrow was long overdue. Both would be appalled by Prime Minister Anthony Eden's bungled attempt in November 1956 to retake the Suez Canal by military means – as were many who belonged to the Liberal elite of 'Our Age',[93] such as their close friend within the British diplomatic corps Sir Frank Roberts, then British ambassador to Yugoslavia.[94]

Orovida Pissarro

Gordine first met the painter-printmaker Orovida (1893–1968) [Plate 19] in 1928 through her father, the painter Lucien Pissarro (1863–1944). Her paternal grandfather was Camille – the great Impressionist artist. There was talk at the time of Gordine producing a bronze portrait head of Lucien, to whom she had probably been introduced by James Bolivar Manson – a fellow founder member of the Camden Town Group – but the commission fell through.[95]

As a leading member of the club's Hanging Committee, Orovida also helped Gordine exhibit with the Women's International Club in London in February 1929 and February 1934. She was an early visitor to Dorich House, once Gordine began inviting guests, and urged her friends to visit the house and admire the sculptor's latest bronzes.[96] In the summer of 1956 she asked Gordine to produce for her a posthumous portrait head of her father that was to be installed inside the new Pissarro Room at the Ashmolean Museum, Oxford.[97] Presumably, it was around this time that she sat for Gordine's charcoal portrait drawing. Orovida strikes one as rather far removed from conventional standards of feminine pulchritude, and yet Gordine again succeeds in conveying the fact that the painter possessed a powerful and commanding personality. Orovida made no secret of her lesbian inclinations, but she was proud of being her father's daughter and was very pleased indeed with the bronze head of Lucien that Gordine created. She admired Gordine partly for her artistic ability but also because she behaved exactly how inter war White Russian exiles to London were popularly imagined.

Gordine, for example, automatically assumed her bronze of Lucien would take pride of place in the Pissarro Room when it was officially opened in June 1957. However, she was outraged to discover from a curator at the Ashmolean that her bronze would be moved from the room to make way for a portrait head of Camille Pissarro by Paulin owned by the museum. She gave the curator a thorough tongue-lashing, for which Orovida felt she must promptly apologise. She wrote to the hapless curator: 'I well understand that her [Gordine's] display of temperament must have annoyed you, but the head itself is a remarkable likeness. I have had a photograph [of her father Lucien] on my mantelpiece ever since the '20s and I find it [the Gordine head] like it more and more. So do try it in a better place! [the next lines were crossed out] 'Forgive me for this impertinence, but Dora Gordine is her own worst enemy!! Have you read Caryl Brahms's *Bullet in the Ballet* – It's just like that!! Russians are queer to say the least!'[98]

A Bullet in the Ballet, by Caryl Brahms (1901–82) and S.J. Simon (1904–48), was first published in 1938 and is a humorous murder mystery set amidst the perennially chaotic 'Stroganoff' Ballet Company. The plot gently pokes fun at the pretensions of the professional ballet world and broadly caricatures highly strung

Russian/foreign artistic types to appeal to the prejudices of middle class British audience. The noted balletomane, Sir John Drummond, later wrote regarding the vogue for the Ballets Russes:

> Post the First World War, émigré Russians in London were the height of exoticism … Caryl Brahms and S.J. Simon caught the mood at the time in their famous spoof *Bullet in the Ballet* … with its wretched male dancer, known as The Man Who Was No Nijinsky, the constant shouting matches, walk-outs and bankruptcy … All very Russian people would say … meaning … glamorous women, dashing Cossacks [and], throaty, tear-jerking songs.[99]

Gordine performed this persona with energetic arm-waving gusto, much to Orovida's amusement. She and Gordine remained friendly until Orovida's death in 1968.

Professor Charles Storey (1888–1967)

Gordine was probably asked by the long-time president of the Royal Asiatic Society, Sir Richard Winstedt, to draw this Cambridge-trained leading historian of the Arab world for the society's art collection. Professor Storey [Plates 20 and 21] had been a distinguished member of the society for nearly thirty years. Storey had been librarian of the India Office, from 1927 to 1933, whereupon he was elected the Thomas Adams Professor of Arabic at Cambridge University. He held the chair until he retired in 1947 and then devoted himself to the study of Persian literature.[100]

The commission may be related to the fact that in June 1962, at Sir Richard's instigation, Richard Hare was invited to lecture to the society on the subject of eastern elements in Russian porcelain.[101] Richard gave the lecture in January of the following year and Professor Storey was in the appreciative audience.[102] Meanwhile, in October 1962, the professor was present at the Victoria and Albert Museum for a talk Richard Hare gave on the silver and jewellery of the Russian empire.[103]

The society retains a more polished drawing of Professor Storey [Plate 21], while Dorich House Museum holds a sketchier, more tentative version [Plate 20]. The professor very much belonged to the world of 'Establishment' Oxbridge academe, with which Richard was so familiar having studied at Balliol and with his numerous contacts at All Souls.[104] By this period, Richard was a notable academic in his own right: early in 1962 the University of London appointed him the first professor of Russian literature at the School of Slavonic and Eastern European Studies.

Plate 19 Orovida Pissarro
1956
charcoal on paper, 65.5 x 50.5 cm
Dorich House Museum

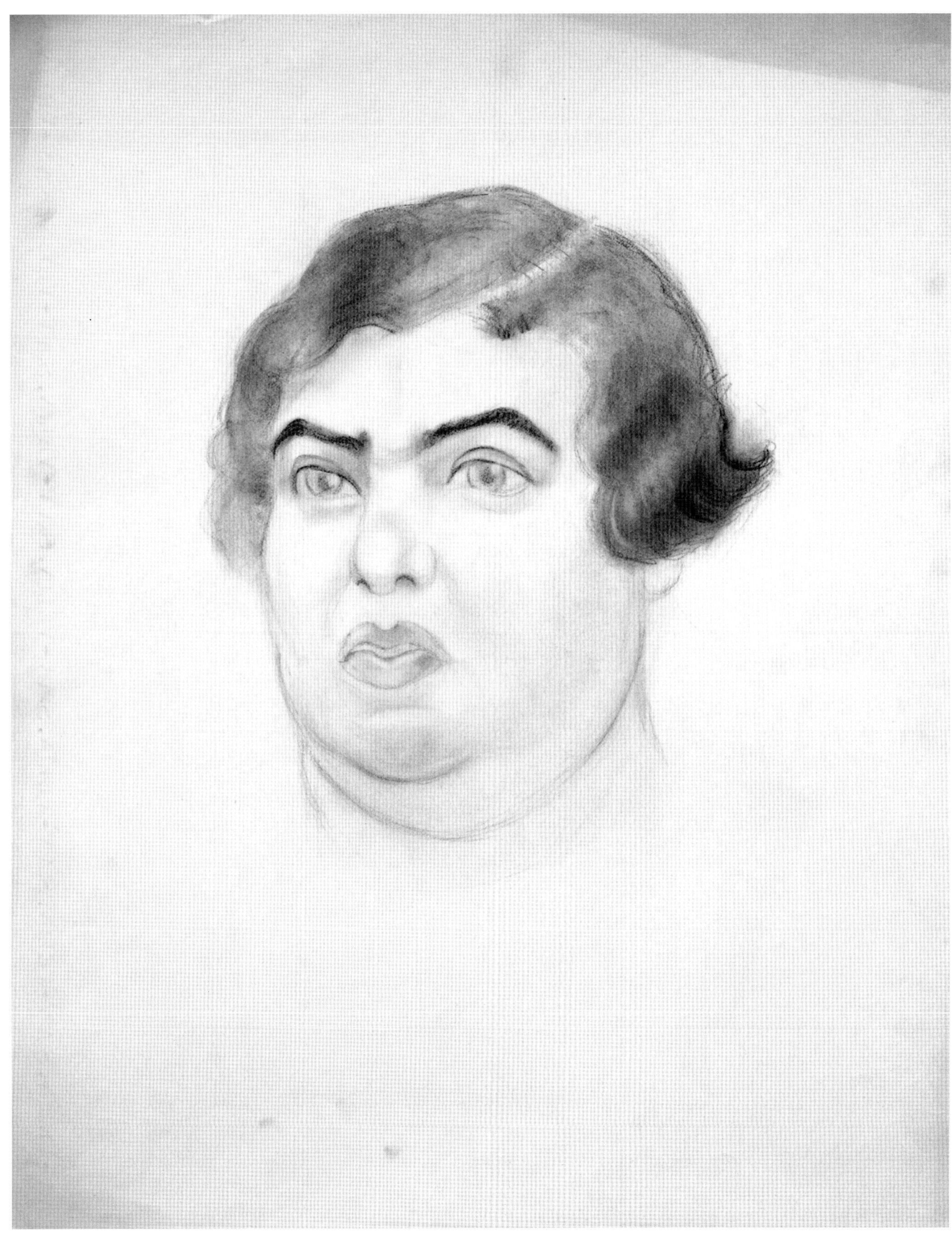

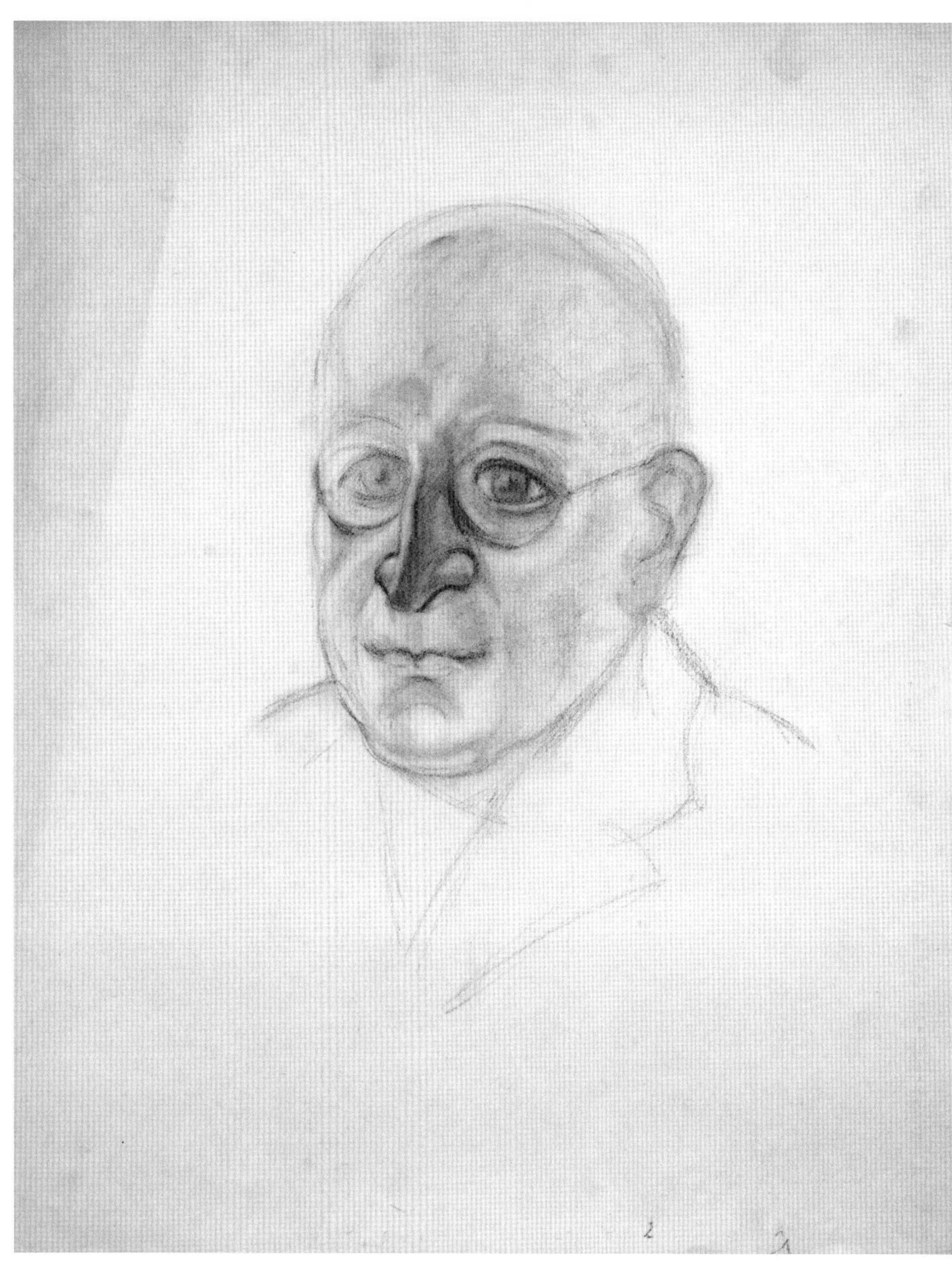

Plate 20 Professor
Charles Storey c.1962
charcoal on paper, 65 x 50 cm
Dorich House Museum

Plate 21 Professor
Charles Storey c.1962
charcoal on paper, 65 x 51 cm
Royal Asiatic Society, London

Portrait drawings of any later sitters have not survived. Richard Hare died suddenly from a heart attack in September 1966 and it would appear a direct consequence of this that Gordine's social circle shrank drastically. She did not exactly become a recluse but fewer and fewer people ventured to Dorich House to see her.[105] Without that direct contact and stimulation, the will to draw dried up. However, her drawings remained important to her and she kept them in good condition despite the increasing dilapidation of Dorich House.

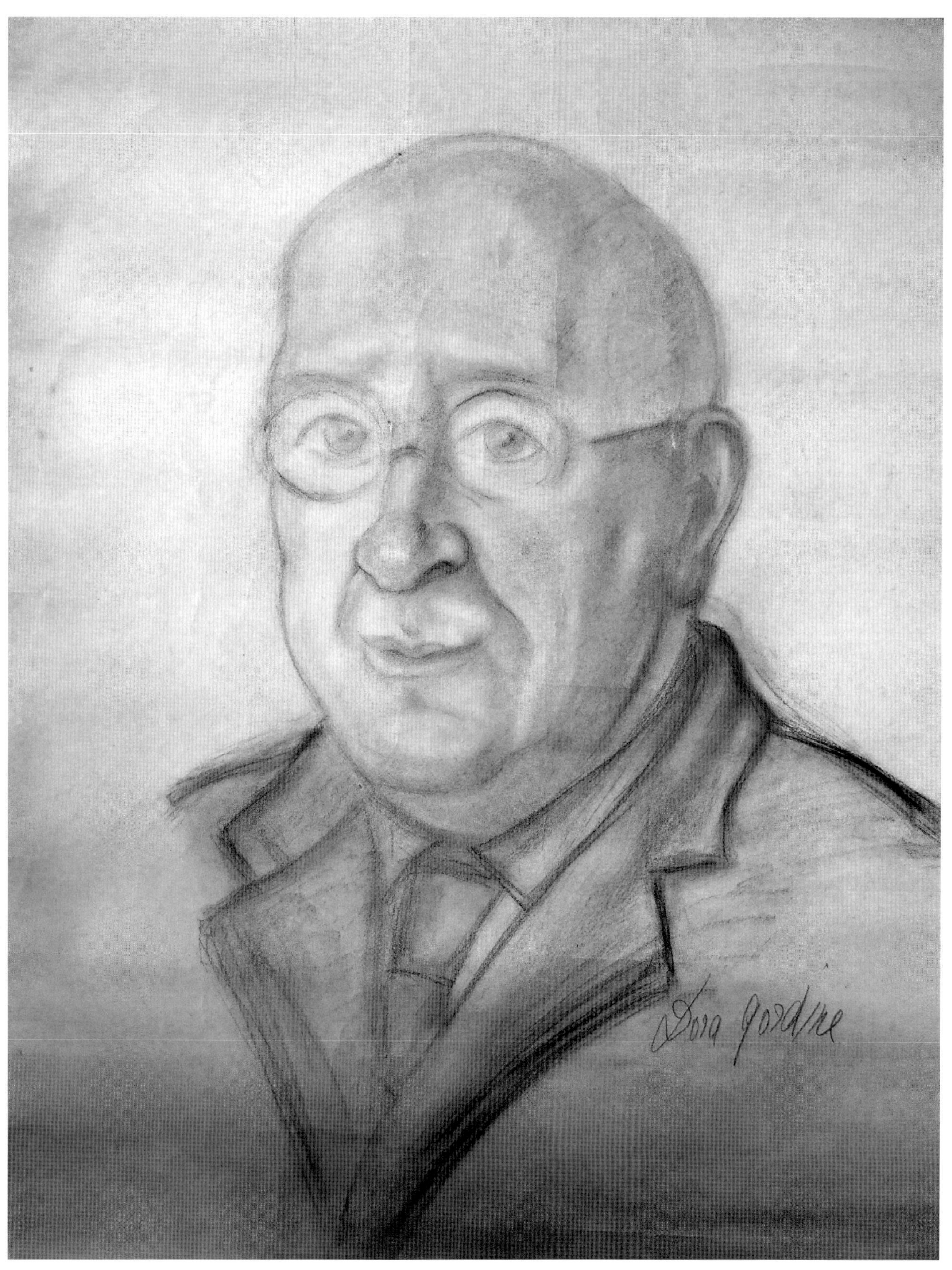
Dora Gordine

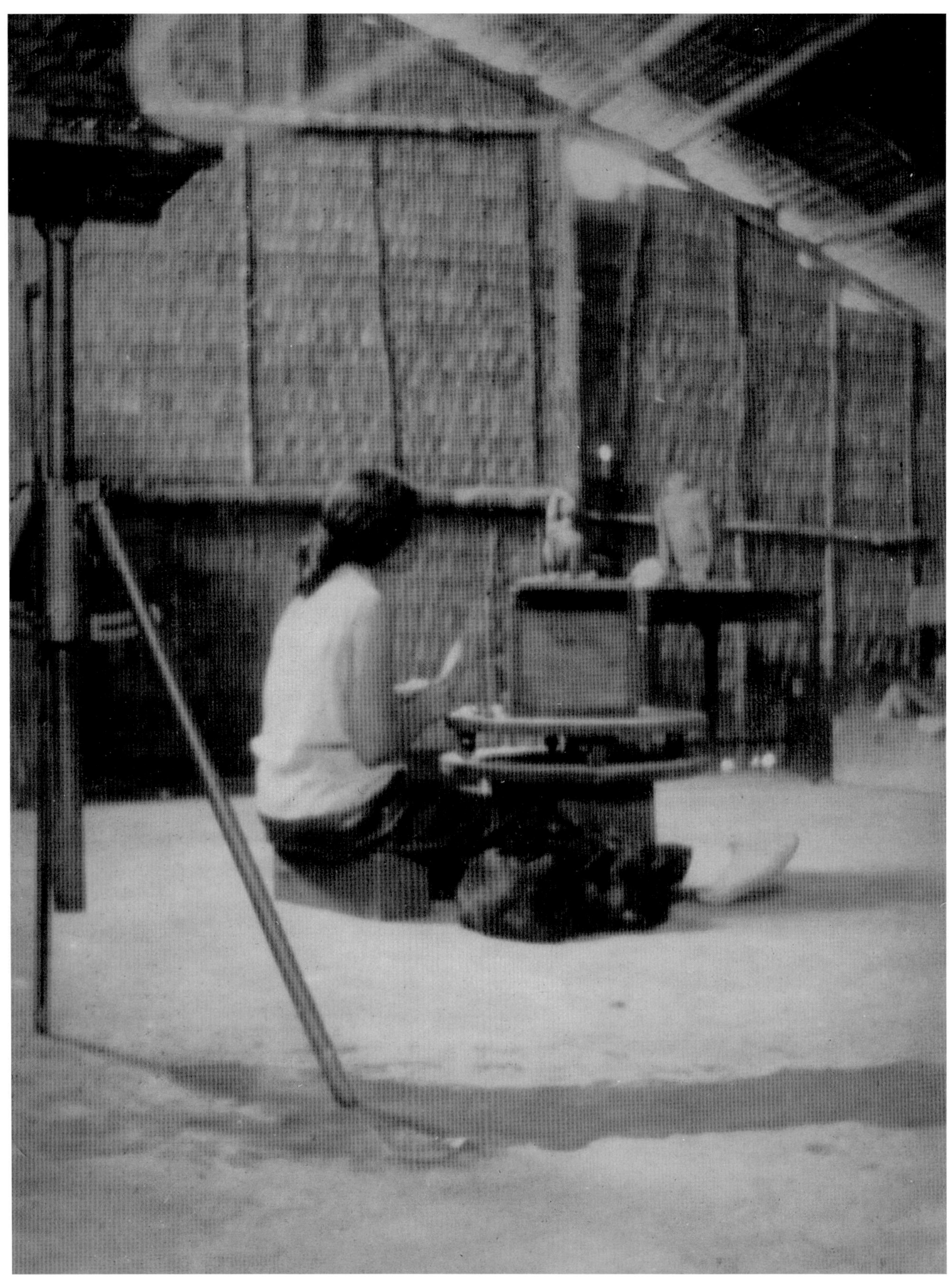

DRAWINGS OF SOUTHEAST ASIA 1930–35

Fran Lloyd

In January 1930, Dora Gordine arrived in British-ruled Singapore, having sailed from Italy via the Suez Canal.[1] Twenty years later she could still vividly recall the experience:

> When I first went to Singapore, the strongest impression I felt was the extraordinary and characteristic beauty of the Malay, Chinese and Indian races. I was fascinated by the quiet, swaying, graceful, walk of the women with their colourful sarongs glowing against their jet-black hair, so decoratively arranged in sleek coils. I was charmed by their expressive dark eyes and serene flower-like faces. It was all so new to me and such an extreme contrast to the quick, energetic movements of European townspeople and to their subdued clothing and surroundings. Starting from this powerful impression of graceful movement, vital colouring and definite form, I became more and more drawn to the artistic expressiveness of Far Eastern people.[2]

Gordine was to live and travel in Southeast Asia for the next five years and to produce numerous figurative drawings, paintings and sculptures in response to her new environment, including a commission of five bronze 'racial heads' and a nude male Caucasian torso for the recently built Municipal Buildings in Singapore. She also developed an intense interest in the culture of the region, and of nearby China and India which she visited. Whilst Gordine was not alone in her fascination with Southeast Asia at this time – indeed it had become a subject of great interest for writers such as Somerset Maugham and George Orwell – it

Plate 22 Dora Gordine at work inside her attap (palm) leaf studio, Johor Bahru, Johor, Malaysia, July 1931
Image courtesy of Archives and Special Collections, University of New York at Buffalo, NY

was still extremely unusual for a European woman artist to choose to settle in the region and unprecedented that one should receive a commission for public sculpture.[3]

The fascination with non-western subjects has a long history in European art and literature. Since at least the eighteenth century it has been closely aligned with the power of the colonial gaze, with empire, and the often interlinked practices of ethnographic and physiognomic studies that sought to classify and fix the 'other' according to race and ethnicity. In particular, much has been written on the various ways in which western artists have consciously or unconsciously perpetuated images of the oriental 'other' as, among other things, passive, childlike, 'primitive', or exotic beings, set apart from the spaces of modernity.[4]

By the time Gordine arrived in Singapore she had already established her reputation in Europe as an accomplished, young artist specialising in so called 'exotic' subjects.[5] These included the bronze head of Chia-Chu Chang, later known as the *Chinese Philosopher* (1925–26), shown to great acclaim at the Salon des Tuileries in Paris in 1926, and 'ethnic' heads such as *Guadeloupe Head* (1926–28) and *Breton Head* (1926–28) shown alongside the voluptuous life-size *Javanese Dancer* (1927) and the *Walking Male Torso* (1927–28) at the Leicester Galleries, London in October 1928. The critics similarly praised her *African Head* shown at the Salon des Tuileries in June 1929 and her 'Mongolian and exotic heads' shown at the Galérie Flechtheim in Berlin in September of the same year.[6]

In the context of British and French imperialism, and the increasing concern with racial purity, most evident in National Socialist Germany in the 1920s, representation of such ethnic types raises questions about racial stereotyping, and the power of the objectifying imperial gaze that assumes intellectual and technological superiority over the exotic or racial other. Such questions are complex, especially in an age of competitive international empire exhibitions, the marked growth of cosmopolitan centres, and increased travel – where numerous artists, writers and collectors also consciously turned to non-western cultures as a potential source of revitalising or, in some cases, breaking free of European conventions. Questions of racial or ethnic stereotyping are particularly complex in the case of Gordine who, in terms of her émigré status in Europe, her unfixed nationality, her undeclared Jewish birth, and her positioning as a woman sculptor drawing directly from the life model, opens up a number of potential points of identification with her non-western sitters.

Strikingly, prior to her arrival in Singapore, writers ascribed the strength of Gordine's works and, in particular, the powerful reworking of the male and female nude in the Caucasian *Walking Male Torso* and *Javanese Dancer* to her background as an exotic Russian-born artist. Writing in February 1928, the critic Gerald Reitlinger described her work as having 'a very un-European spirit … in the spirit of classical Buddhist sculpture from India and Japan'. He concluded: 'It is not surprising that a Russian midway between Europe and the East in spirit should have seized it.'[7] Later that year the French critic Lucien Cordier referred to Gordine as an 'Asiatic … caught between the Orient and the West' whose 'strangely elongated eyes bear an unnerving … oriental stillness.'[8] Given such descriptions, it is intriguing to conjecture that Gordine's cross-border positioning as European-cum-oriental, together with her recently arrived status and highly acclaimed professional standing, made her an ideal artist to create a modern but sympathetic representation of the multiple ethnicities of Singapore that was aligned with the British authorities' political and economic need to create a more coherent identity for the region.

Although Gordine may have had an inkling of the possibility of a commission for the new building through Roland Braddell whom she had probably met in London in 1928, she put herself in a potentially unpredictable situation by choosing to leave a successful artistic career in Europe to go to British Malaya and the Unfederated States of Southeast Asia in 1930. Whilst America and Britain were hit by the catastrophe of the Wall Street Crash of October 1929, and Paris, like Germany, was experiencing the rise of antisemitism, British Malaya was experiencing other tensions before the impact of the crash was felt.[9] Uppermost, from the British perspective, was the increasing concern for the political stability of the area with its many distinct ethnicities. At this point in time the population of Malaya stood at 4.4 million, of which the 'Malay Races', including the Javanese and 'aboriginal Dayaks', comprised 45 percent, the Chinese 39 percent, Indians 14 percent and White Europeans 0.4 percent (17,964).[10] Malays living on the peninsula, for example, did not perceive themselves as Malayan but as the subjects of one of the ten Muslim sultans. The Chinese community, predominately Tao and Confucian with some Christians and Buddhists, was divided racially between the Hokkien from southern China and the Hakka from the north, and politically between supporters of Chiang Kai-shek's Nationalists and Mao Zedong's Communists who were fighting a civil war on mainland China.[11] The Indian community was also divided between prosperous middle class merchants, Sikhs – who provided men for the police force – and predominately Hindu Tamils from southern India who immigrated to Malaya in large numbers from 1900 to the late 1920s to work on the rubber plantations.[12]

Aware of the growth of independence movements and the increased threat of imperial Japan, Sir Cecil Clementi (1875–1947), former governor of Hong Kong, was appointed as the high commissioner of the Federated Malay States and governor of the Straits Settlements in February 1930, specifically to rationalize the administrative system of British Malaya and to devolve greater powers to native Malay officials. He was equally keen to promote a sense of Malay national

overleaf left
Plate 23 Malay Woman Walking (seen from behind) c.1930–32
charcoal on paper, 66 x 54 cm
Dorich House Museum

overleaf right
Plate 24 Head of a Malay Fisherman c.1930–31
charcoal on paper, 66 x 56 cm
Dorich House Museum

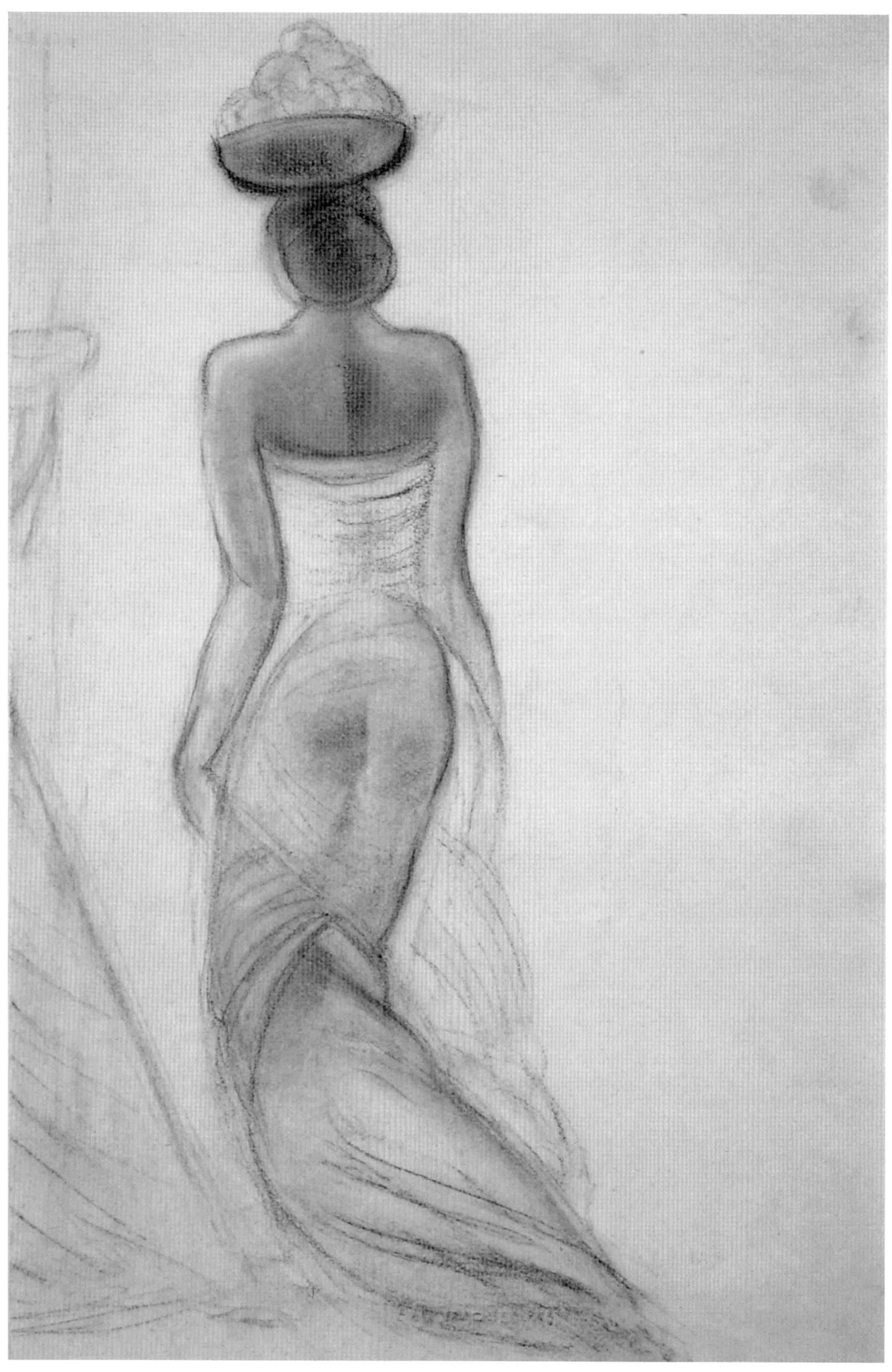

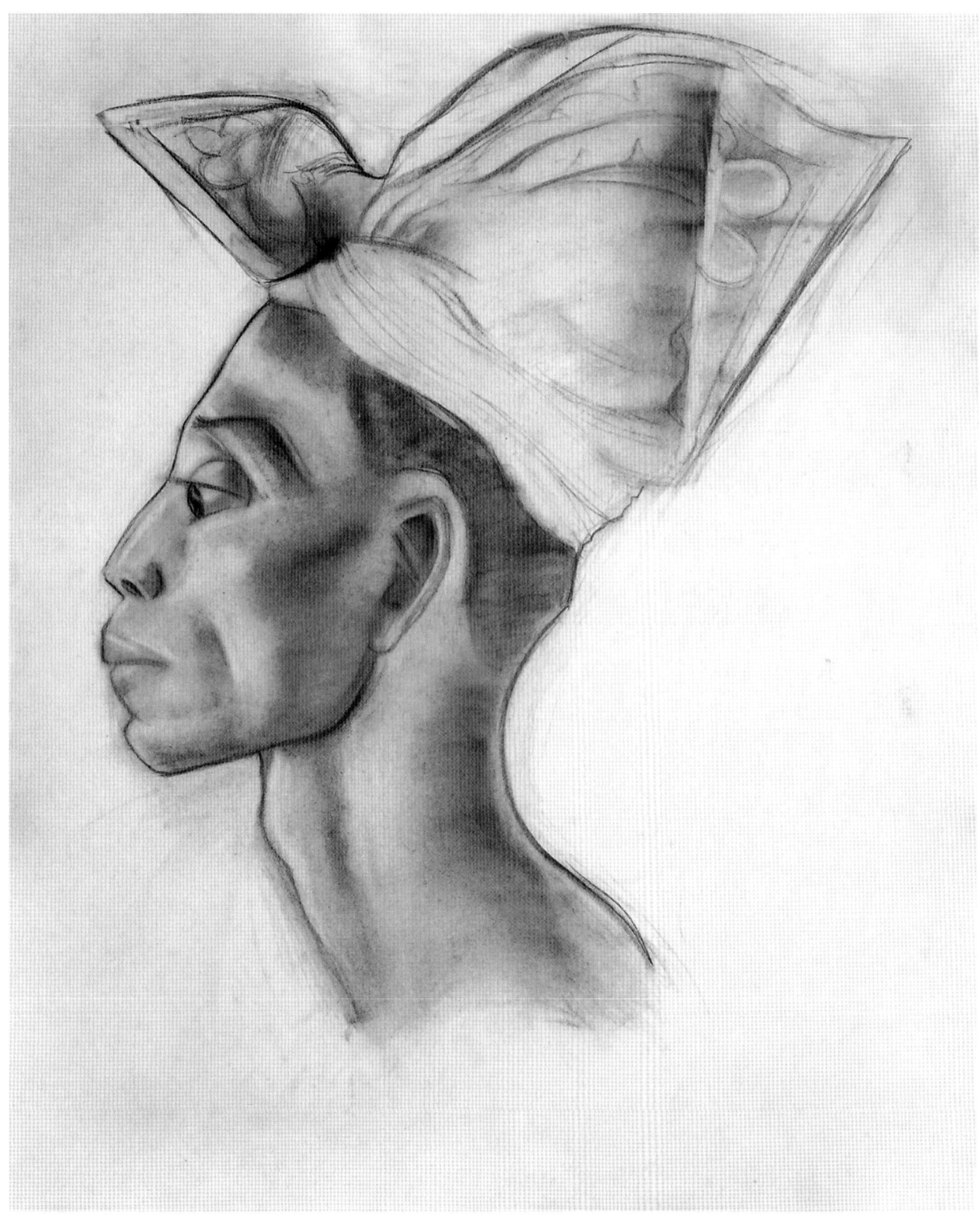

identity without alienating the Chinese and Indian immigrant communities who were suspicious of Malay nationalism.[13]

By 1930, when Gordine arrived in Singapore, the island had a population of just over 445,000, including a large European ex-pat community. Rather than settling in the fashionable metropolis, however, Gordine decided to live just across the Straits of Johor in Johor Bahru, the capital of the Unfederated Malay State of Johor, on the southern tip of the Malay peninsula.[14] Johor was ruled by the sultan of Johor, Sir Ibrahim ibn abu Bakar (1873–1959),[15] who acknowledged British authority on defence and foreign policy through a general advisor from the Malay civil service, but otherwise had near absolute power.[16] Linked to Singapore by the Johor-Singapore Causeway – completed in 1923 – the then small town of Johor Bahru had a population of just over 21,000, which included British residents of the so-called 'official class' numbering no more than 120.[17] Whether for economic reasons or otherwise, Gordine elected for a more rural setting and established a studio made from attap (palm) leaves on the outskirts of Johor Bahru [Plate 22].

A series of drawings from this period shows Gordine's fascination with the diverse communities in the region characterised by the variations in facial features, skin colour, and dress that articulated differences of ethnicity, religious affiliation and social position in a highly stratified and gendered colonial society. Her drawings, like those of many sculptors in the period, focus on portraying the figure or face, with rare indications of the surrounding environment. *Malay Woman Walking* (c. 1930–32) [Plate 23], for example, suggests a street drawing that represents the figure in movement while engaged in everyday activity. Gordine's characteristic use of an assured outline on the body and accompanying shading gives the figure solidity while the finer charcoal lines sensuously articulate the flow of drapery and the rhythm of graceful movement. By comparison, the detailed studio portrait of *Head of a Malay Fisherman* (c. 1930–32) [Plate 24], explores the pronounced facial bone structure of the male model through attentively modulated shading. Alert to the status and gender of the sitter, the drawing carefully represents the elaborately knotted and patterned headscarf that acts simultaneously as a marker of his trade – as one of a long line of local fishermen respected for their skill – and of his masculinity. In keeping with her previous 'ethnic' heads with their striking silhouette shapes, Gordine transforms the fisherman into an iconic image that resembles the hieratic royal heads of King Akhenaton or Queen Nefertiti of ancient Egypt which, as the *Observer* critic P.G. Konody noted in 1928, she certainly knew from her time in Berlin.[18] A parallel can also be drawn with the powerful and compelling charcoal portraits of the late 1920s by the French artist Anna Quinquaud (1890–1984) [Fig. 10] who was interested in the portrayal of 'exotic' subjects, particularly those of Mauritania,

Senegal and Niger (the French African colonies), where she travelled, in a break with tradition, after winning the second Grand Prix de Rome in 1924.[19]

In August 1930, seven months after her arrival, Gordine gave her first public interview to the *Straits Times of Singapore*, which provides a great insight into her perceptions of Malaya and its inhabitants. After recounting a brief history of the artist's work to date alongside an image of the piece now known as the *Chinese Philosopher*, the reporter noted:

> In Europe she said she always felt cramped and thought of going to Africa, or the East. Later she decided on the East for here she felt sure she could find ideal types to model … She said that the naturally graceful movements of the Eastern peoples fascinated her. She contrasted the efforts the average European has to make to maintain a dignified appearance and the quiet and naturally dignified bearing of the Eastern.

Fig.10 Anna Quinquaud, *Mauritanian Woman*, 1927–28, charcoal on paper, 90 x 75 cm, Private Collection, London, Image: Dorich House Museum

The interview goes on to refer to the 'figures of the Tamils [who] are ideal for her work, for their excellent proportions and grace of line express a beauty unknown in Europe. Work is a little difficult here, she admitted, for she has not yet become accustomed to the heat. She has completed two casts, a Chinese and a Hindu. She has four more under way and will give the casts to be fashioned in bronze by the Municipality [of Singapore]. She is at present studying Hindu classic poses in the nude.'

Notably, 'speaking generally of the art of sculpture she said: "Few people really understand it, for they do not know where to search for its beauty … Could the monuments of the Golden Hindu [Buddhist] era be seen in Borobudhur[20] [on Java] and the art treasures of Angkor [in Cambodia] ever have been produced in the narrow confines of a teeming city? I am enthralled by the East, fascinated by its movement, but cannot help deploring the western influences which tend to kill its natural beauty."' [21]

Several things are striking in this account. First, Gordine's confidence that she will find 'ideal types to model' in Southeast Asia (presumably based in part on her knowledge of oriental art collections in the museums of Paris, London and Berlin);[22] second, her choice of Asia over the colonial spaces of West and East Africa which had attracted many of her contemporaries, including several artist acquaintances from London and Paris; and third, her keen interest in and knowledge of her new surroundings, which was allegedly relatively uncommon during the period.[23] It is also apparent that the Singapore municipal commissioners had already asked Gordine to provide six bronzes for the sum of £1,000 ($20,000) for the interior of the recently completed Municipal Buildings (now the former parliament building),[24] which included five 'ethnic heads', representative of the races living within British Malaya. These were *Mongolian Head* (produced prior to her arrival in Singapore and exhibited in Paris in 1928), *Chinese Head* (also known as *Kwa Nin – Chinese Lady of Peace*),[25] *Hindu Head*, *Malay Head* and *Javanese Head*, modelled in her Johor studio from 1930 to 1931.[26]

Gordine produced numerous portrait drawings of Tamil males which include two studies for the *Hindu Head* (c. 1930–31) later shown in 1933 at the Leicester Galleries in London. The arresting charcoal studio portrait [Plate 25] depicts a young handsome and muscular male with strong clean-cut features. The drawing has a freshness and vitality based on direct observation from the model. The finished bronze, by comparison, retains the same angular, simplified pose, but the head is softened by the rich, golden brown patina of the surface and the unfocused gaze is more distant and hence less animated. If, in part, this is a result of the physical translation of the portrait into clay and of the subsequent casting process, it also exemplifies the distinctive gravity and dignity that Gordine sought to achieve for her sitters in the final bronze works.

Gordine rarely titled her drawings, and very few record the name of the sitter. The numerous male and female portrait drawings of Malay, Chinese and Tamil sitters, amongst others, nonetheless embody an intense interest in the physical and psychological character of each individual. Her diverse drawings of Chinese females, for instance, include portraits of children, of young fashionable women sporting the latest hairstyle alongside a more conventional mandarin collar dress [Plate 26], and of those wearing European style dress.

Gordine must have represented an unusual figure within the European hierarchy of status in British Malaya. On the one hand she was clearly 'exotic' and foreign, while equally she could be identified as part of the colonial ruling class that exercised political and economic power. Moreover, just over a month after her *Straits Times* interview, on 18 September 1930, Gordine married the British-born Dr George Herbert Garlick (1886–1958), then deputy chief medical officer of the Johor Medical Service and personal doctor to Sultan Ibrahim of Johor, at the Registry Office, Singapore. Her standing is evident by the guests, who included, amongst others, the Tungku Ampuan, the sultan of Johor's elder sister,

Plate 25 Hindu Head (Head of Tamil) c.1930–32
charcoal on paper, 66 x 56 cm
Dorich House Museum

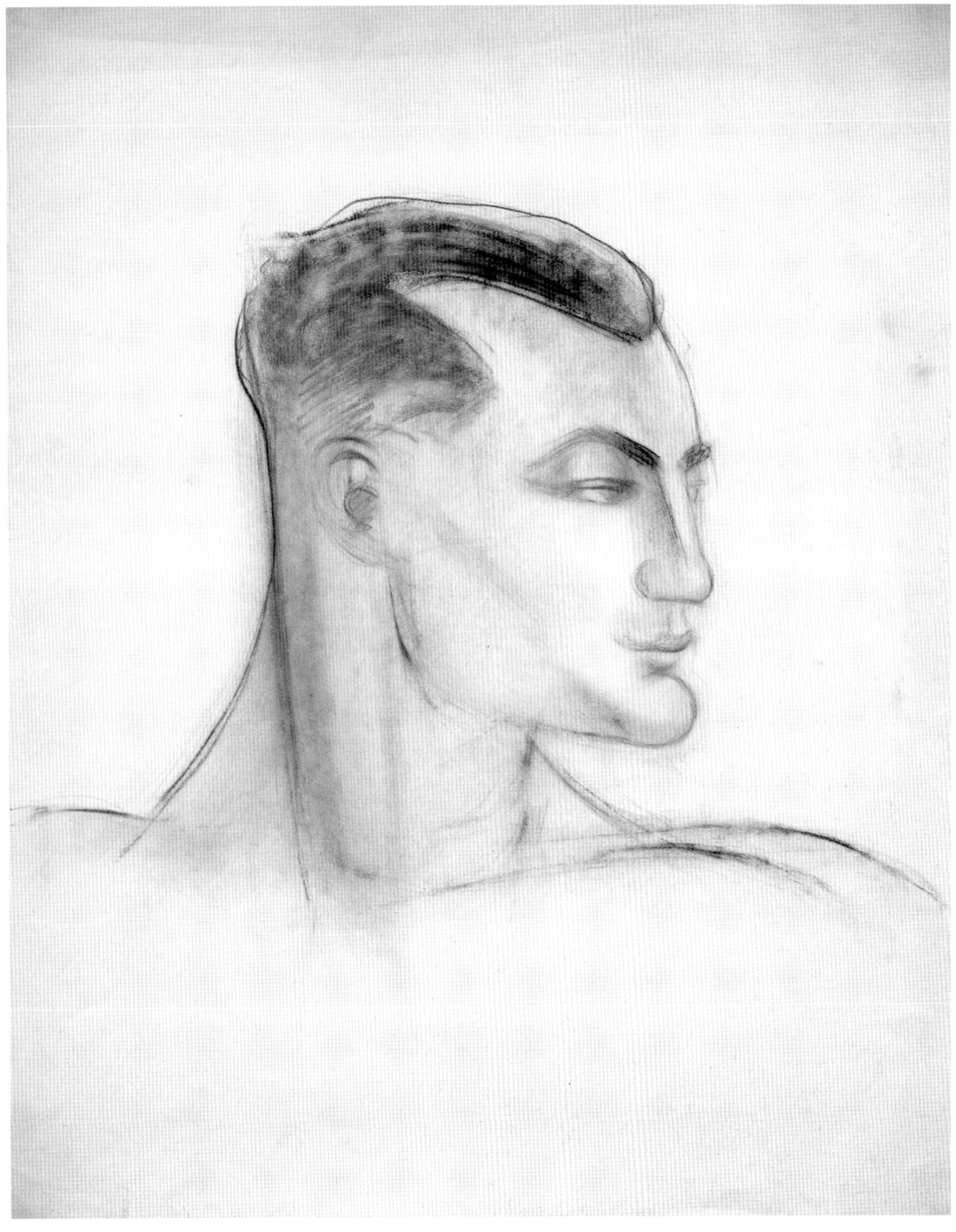

Tungku Abu Bakar, the sultan's second son, and Ungku Abdul Aziz.[27] Meanwhile, shortly after her marriage, Gordine made a very influential friend in Richard Winstedt (1878–1966), the recently appointed British 'general advisor' to Sultan Ibrahim.

Throughout her time in Southeast Asia, Gordine produced many striking drawings of female nudes which, in keeping with her contemporaries in Europe, were the favoured subject of male and female artists alike. The majority of the black charcoal drawings depict the reclining or standing nude, or the more sketchy movements of dancers. In general, the emphasis is on the body rather than the face, including a number of drawings of torsos that concentrate on the weightiness of the rounded female body. Others employ red charcoal which, in common with the manner of French sculptors Maillol and Despiau [Figs. 2 and 4] is used to great effect to provide depth in the curvaceous female bodies. Notably, although Gordine produced few drawings of the male nude, these were exclusively rendered in black charcoal or pencil.

Two recently discovered photographs of the Johor Bahru studio, taken around July 1931, enable insights into Gordine's working practices at the time. One shows the raised turntable and chair that her models occupied during portrait sittings. As the critic D.S. McColl observed in the catalogue introduction to Gordine's November 1938 exhibition at the Leicester Galleries, where drawings were exhibited alongside her sculpture for the first and only time, 'after testing general character in a preliminary drawing', she 'takes no measurements and uses no calipers', but 'works as a painter does, by the eye'.[28] This process, as Gordine and several of her latter models commented upon, was an intense and intimate one that took place over a period of time.

By July 1931, as the studio photographs reveal, Gordine was working on two nude sculptures alongside the ethnic heads: her second large male torso later entitled *Male Torso/Dyak* (1932, bronze, Dorich House Museum), and the much smaller female figure of *Cingalese Girl* (1932, bronze, Dorich House Museum). Both nudes, based upon local sitters, were to receive much attention when first shown in London, the heart of empire, in the late 1930s.[29] From the existing drawings for both works, it is clear that Gordine strictly adhered to certain social conventions in Singapore that accorded with the gender of the sitter. For the female figure, she worked from a nude model and, for the male figure, from a seminude model.

The two charcoal sketches for *Cingalese Girl* represent the nude semi-reclining sitter in the final resolved pose, in this case, seen from the back and resting on one arm. Without recourse to shading, the simple outline drawing of the figure emphasises the shape of the body, as does the final sculpture that was later photographed c. 1935 in the centre of a large pond in the grounds of the Round

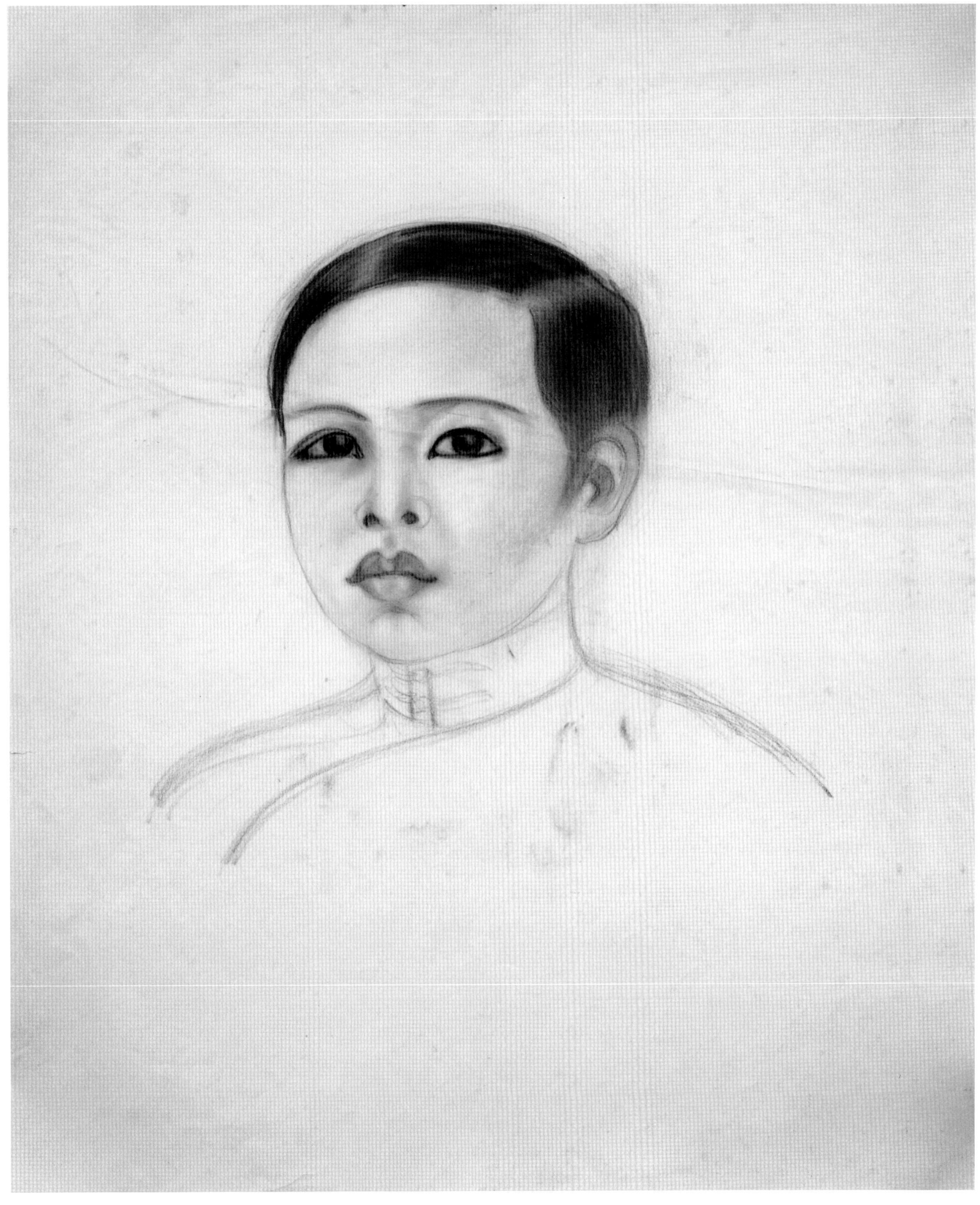

House, built by Dr Garlick, after Gordine had returned to London for good.[30]

Concentrated on the north-eastern coast of Borneo (now the states of Sarawak and Brunei), in the south, and in the eastern highlands,[31] the animist dyaks/iban engaged in highly ritualized warfare, which involved headhunting as a means of warding off evil spirits and as a fertility rite. By the 1930s the British authorities had largely managed to prohibit headhunting and by all accounts the dyaks were generally well regarded as honourable and hardworking, as well as being admired for their physical strength and dignity.[32]

According to Gordine, in an account broadcast on BBC Radio in January 1945, the model for *Dyak* was a 'wild head-hunter from Borneo' who had been brought to Singapore Island to help clear the jungle. She also dramatically states that: 'I had to lock him up in his hut at night because he had never slept under a roof till he was brought to Singapore … I began a magnificent statue and I was so afraid he might runaway before I finish[ed] it. He also did unexpected things, like catching snakes and eating them, but once I got to know him I was charmed by his simple, kindly and harmonious nature.' [33]

While this uncomfortable account, undoubtedly meant to shock and entice BBC listeners, is a classic example of overdetermined exoticism that reproduces the stereotype of the male savage, the four existing drawings – of which three are reproduced here – represent a very different figure [Plates 27–29]. The broad-shouldered male sitter, whether standing, walking, or kneeling, is depicted as a powerful and monumental figure through the dramatic use of shading and attention to muscularity. Set near to the picture plane, and therefore closer in proximity to the viewer, the emphasis is on the solidity of each of the figures. This is heightened in the walking figure, with the long headscarf just visible on the left, by the almost architectonic simplification of the body into planes which recalls Gordine's many descriptions of the power of Buddhist and Hindu temple sculpture.

From January to March 1931, prior to commencing these drawings, Gordine had travelled through Malaya, the Dutch East Indies (Java and Bali), French Indo-China (Cambodia), Siam (now Thailand) and British-controlled Burma (see page 70). On 4 February 1931 the *Bangkok Times* reported that Gordine 'who has been placed by European critics with Maillol as one of the three greatest European sculptors' had arrived in the city on the SS *Kuala*. The newspaper subsequently printed an article on Gordine's visit to Angkor Wat in northwest Cambodia, 'Angkor: Impressions of a Sculptor', in which she is recorded as saying:

I have spent a week here and have seen everything, and yet nothing … The fact that impresses me, above all others, is the use of sculpture and architecture as one art … Many of the sculptures are so pure, so

Plate 27 Kneeling Malay Male c.1931–32
charcoal on paper, 66 x 56 cm
Dorich House Museum

overleaf left
Plate 28 Standing Malay Male c.1931–32
charcoal on paper, 66 x 56 cm
Dorich House Museum

overleaf right
Plate 29 Standing Malay Male c.1931–32
charcoal on paper, 66 x 56 cm
Dorich House Museum

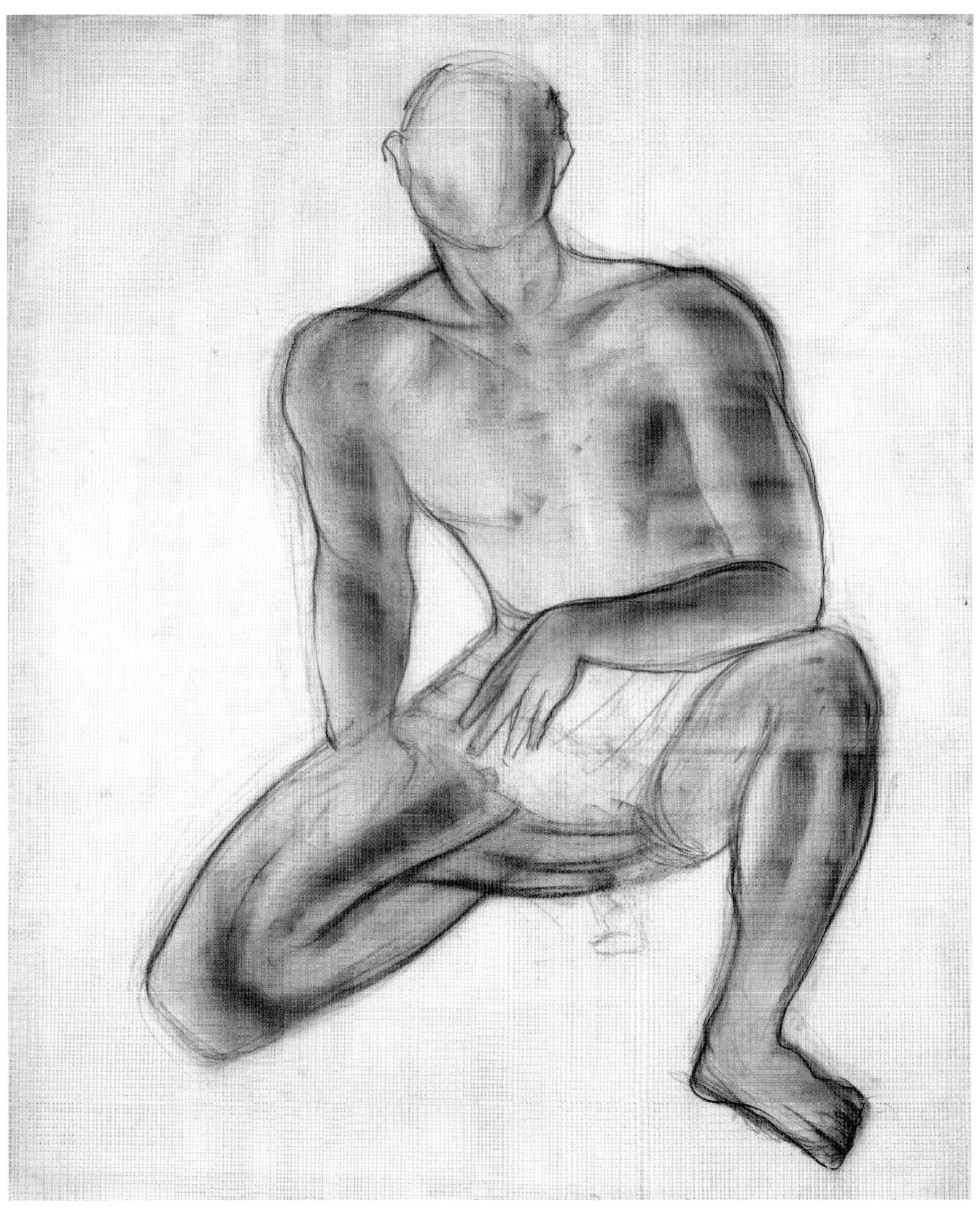

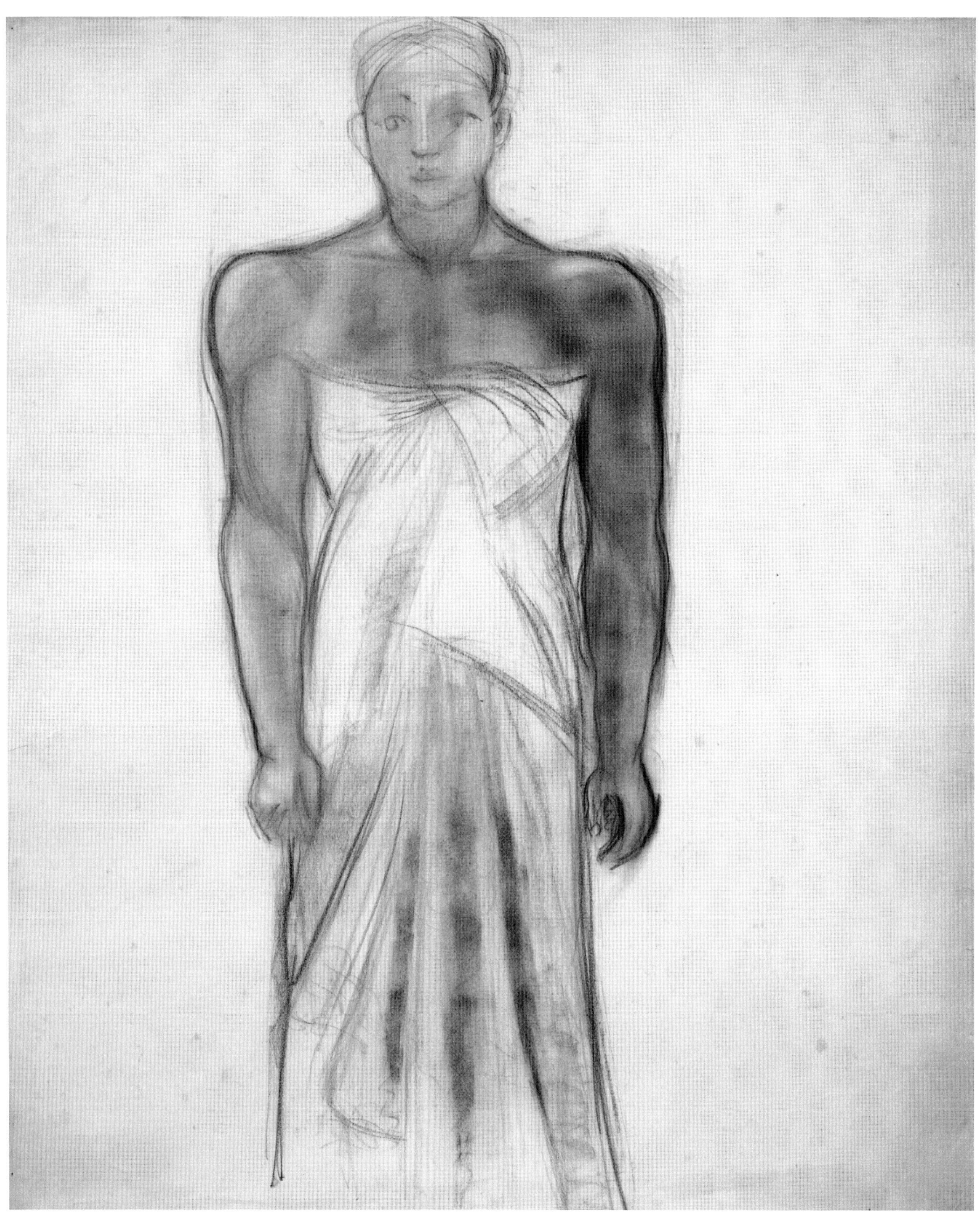

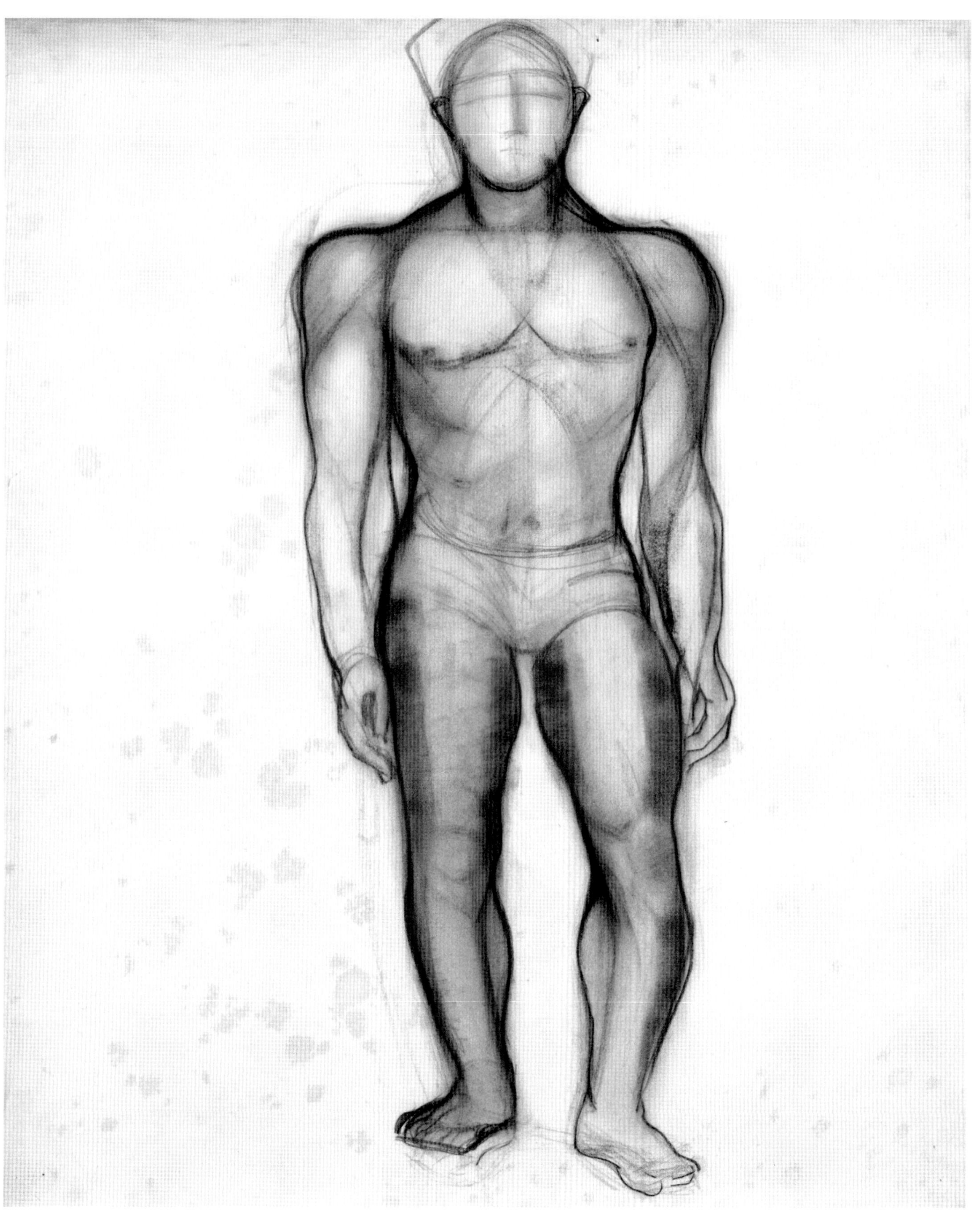

monumental, so powerful in form and refined in expression, as to be unrivalled anywhere … I recognise, after what I have seen, that no descriptions begin to be adequate.[34]

If the final bronze torso of the indigenous dyak/iban is seen as the result of her engagement with Southeast Asian culture, both past and present, it is also a highly significant visual and symbolic counterpart to the bronze *Waking Male Torso* previously purchased for the Municipal Buildings in 1931. According to the *Straits Times* of February 1931, this 'over-life size torso will stand in the middle of the space there which overlooks the sea. The torso, which was taken from a Caucasian model, shows the ideal male form with broad shoulders and small hips.'[35] In the context of British Singapore, *Dyak* subverts this imperial image and represents a new ideal of equal dignity and power.

In a strange reversal that acts as a reminder of the interconnected but differently positioned spaces of empire, when *Dyak* was exhibited in London at the Leicester Galleries in November 1933, Arthur Symons, who had been a leading decadent poet of the 1890s, immediately responded to his knowledge of its Southeast Asian origins, describing the figure as:

magnificently masculine and there is an intense simplicity and that intensity of life which seems to exist in every limb. She has given him neither head nor feet. What she gives is the body of a primitive animal, ready to seize his prey like a wild beast, virile and capable of any violent action. And you feel the solidity of that immense weight, what force and reality, what sudden arrested life [is] in those long arms and furiously clenched hands. When one has all these qualities, then the sculpture becomes neither ancient nor modern but a great force of sculpture, neither of today nor of tomorrow.[36]

In the same article Symons also commented on Gordine's seated female figure *Pagan*, which he saw as possessing a 'deeply erotic appeal … perfectly self-contained, and obeying no laws save those which it derives from its own sense of harmony and perfection.'[37]

The impact of Gordine's visit to the monumental Khmer sculpture at Angkor Wat (c. 12th century CE) and the stone carvings at the Buddhist temple complex at Borobudhur (6–9th century CE) in Java, Indonesia are evident in the three surviving large-scale drawings Gordine produced for the bronze entitled *Pagan* c. 1932–33. One depicts the figure from the front, the second the back view of the model [Plate 30], and the third is a series of sketches on one sheet exploring hand gestures and facial features. In the first two, the rounded female figure

Plate 30 Study for Pagan
(seen from behind)
c.1932–33
charcoal on paper, 66 x 56 cm
Dorich House Museum

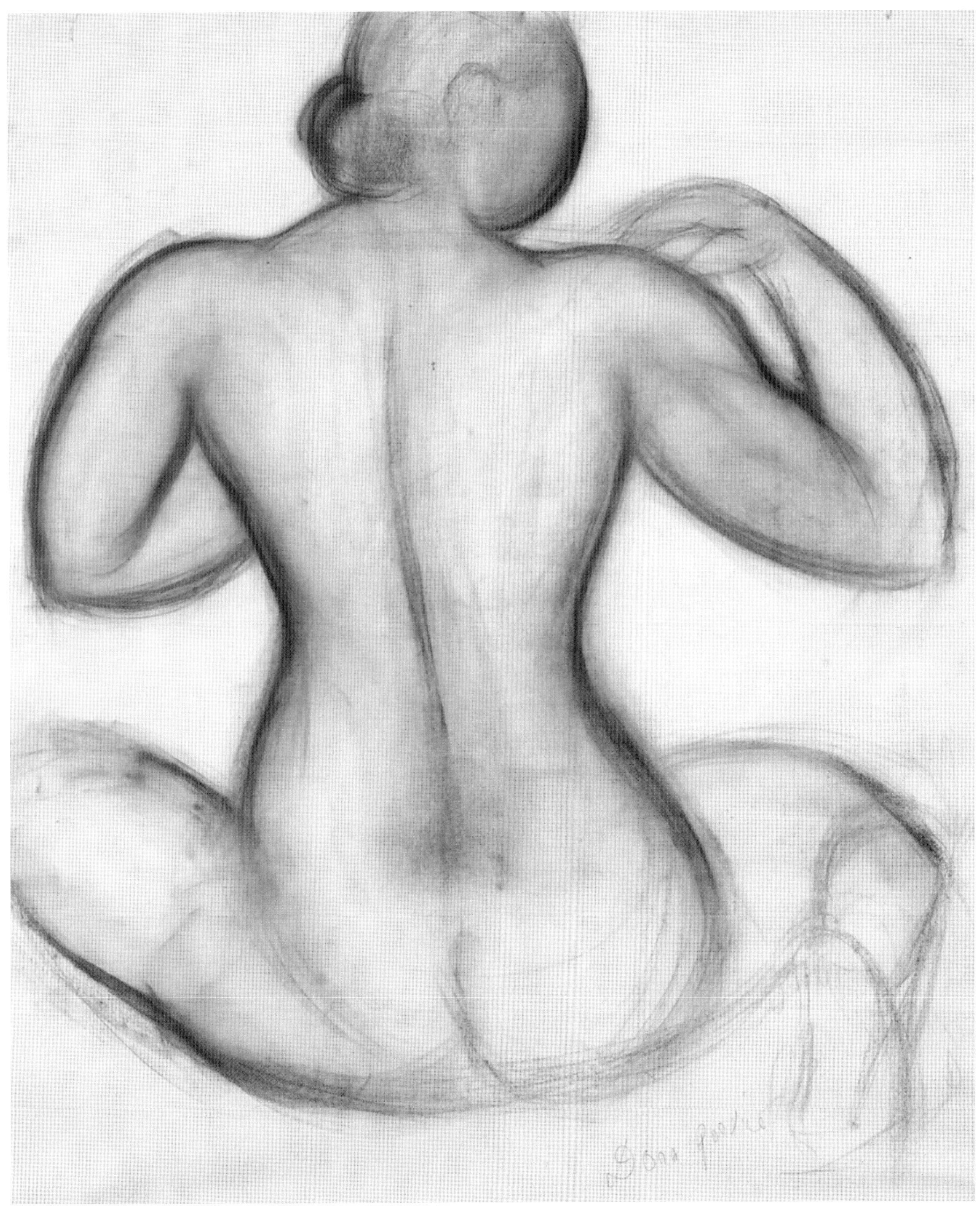

fills the entire page with the assured outline and sparsely used shading adding weight and solidity to the form. The scale of this ample figure indicates a new monumentality in Gordine's work that is shared with several of her European contemporaries from this time, including Eric Kennington and Henry Moore [Figs. 7–9].

One of the most unusual Gordine drawings is a red charcoal standing nude figure with a bright yellow necklace and blue hair [Plate 31]. The figure's stance, with the tapering waist and the swing of the hips, suggests a dancer, and she is adorned by blue marks that pick out her nipples and belly button. The rich use of multi-coloured charcoal and pastel crayon is uncharacteristic of Gordine, although the voluptuous body has correspondences with the over-life-size bronze figure of *Iran* (also known as *Goddess of Health*), 1932–33, also initiated in Southeast Asia and first exhibited at the Leicester Galleries in July 1933. Symons was equally taken with the evocative power of this sculpture and wrote in unambiguous terms about the 'savage and barbaric' female who 'overflows with animal life' that reminded him of a woman in Conrad's *Heart of Darkness*, '…[a] colossal body of the fecund and mysterious life.'

In August 1932 Gordine and Dr Garlick sailed from Singapore for France and by September–October 1932 they had moved into 21 rue du Belvédère, Boulogne-Billancourt, Paris, where Gordine completed the sculpture in time for her July exhibition.[38] Gordine exhibited fifteen bronzes at the Leicester Galleries, London, including *Head of a Chinese Lady, Javanese Head, Malay Head* and *Malay Sultana,* the portrait of the strong-willed elder sister of Sultan Sir Ibrahim ibn abu Bakar, also known as the *Tungku Ampuan of Johor*. Once again, her Southeast Asian heads were described in terms that recognised the dignity of subjects by combining an 'outward beauty and strength [with] inward power, grace and feeling.'[39]

In October 1933, Gordine returned to Johor Bahru via Paris. Richard Hare, whom she had first met in London in 1926 and was subsequently to marry after her return to Britain in July 1935, arrived in Singapore in February 1934. In the autumn of 1934–35 Gordine also visited Java and Bali, in the Dutch East Indies, French Indo-China, and then Shanghai and Beijing in the company of Hare. By the time they visited Bali in September 1934, the island was already beginning to become a popular destination for the more adventurous Western European traveller, including the film director Josef von Sternberg, whom Gordine had met in Berlin in September 1929, and who stayed on the island from 1932–33.[40] Gordine was clearly enchanted by the place and produced dozens of drawings of the Balinese, including portraits and charcoal drawings of people encountered in the street, as well as the better known temple dancers [Fig. 11]. Later, reflecting on these works, she spoke about the importance of embodying the 'warmth and

Plate 31 **Standing Female Nude with Blue Hair**

c. 1930–31

red chalk and charcoal on paper, 66 x 56 cm

Dorich House Museum

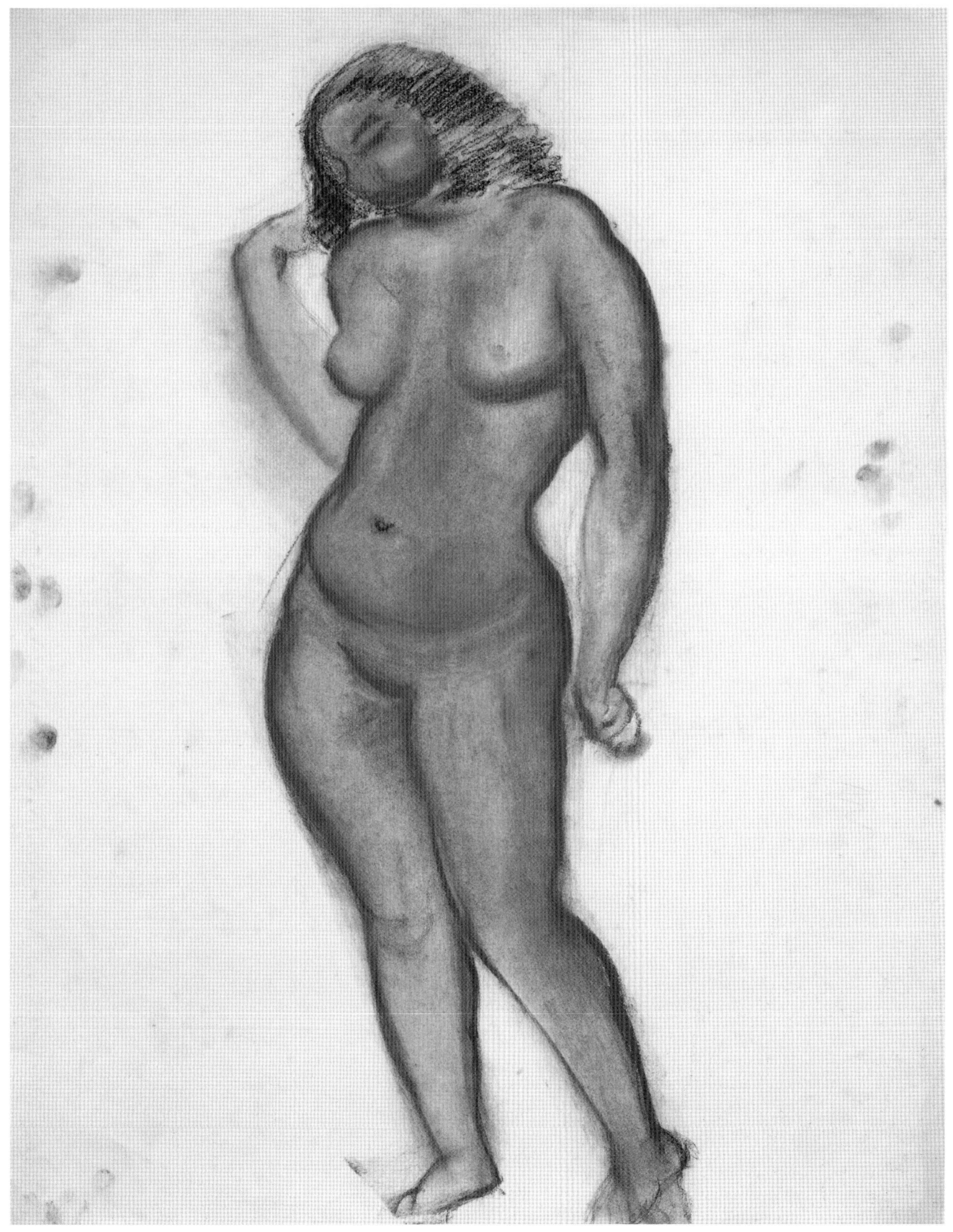

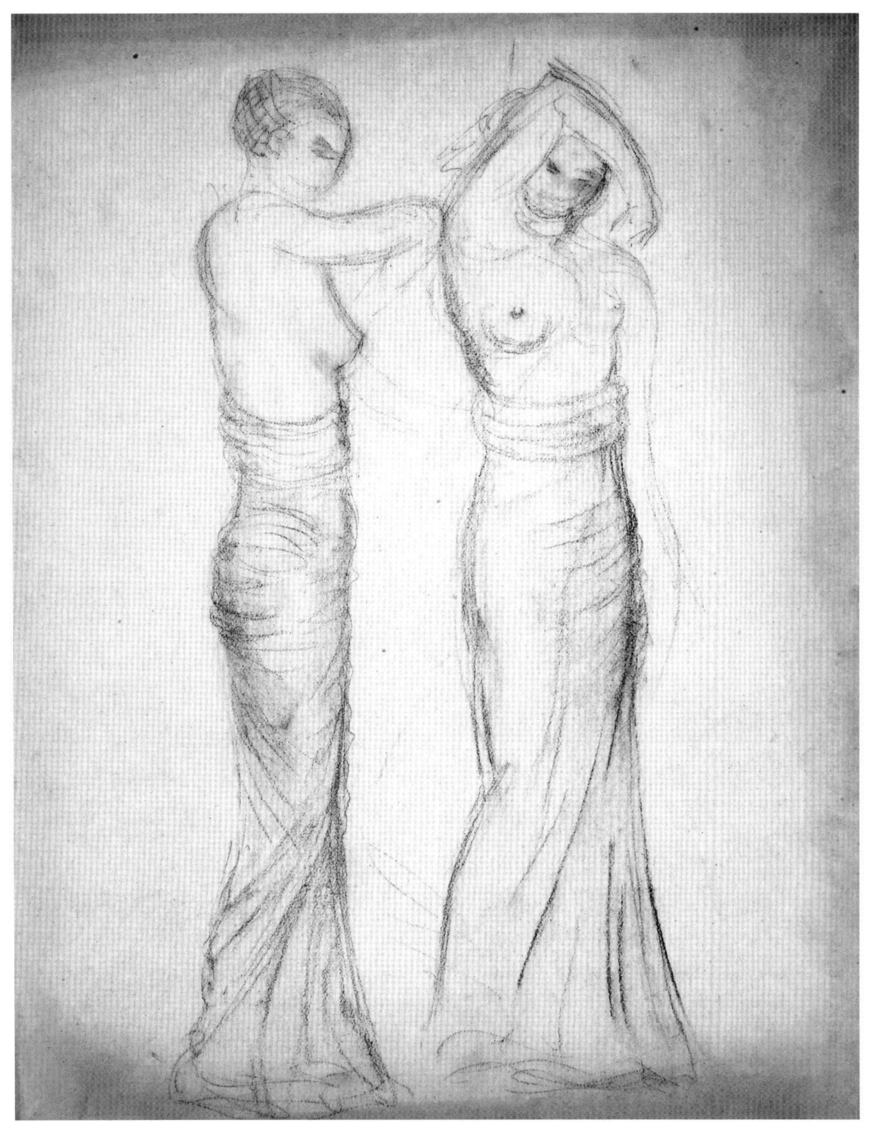

Fig.11 Dora Gordine, Two Balinese Temple Dancers, c. 1934–35, charcoal on paper, 66 x 56 cm, Dorich House Museum

Plate 32 Seated Balinese Woman c.1934
charcoal on paper, 66 x 56 cm
Dorich House Museum

richness of life' through the act of drawing such different sitters [Plate 32].[41]

As Richard Hare wrote to a friend in London, at this time Gordine also 'started painting seriously and [became] deeply absorbed in it.'[42] In 1945, she specifically referred to the Javanese woman who sat for two of these oil paintings [Plate 1, frontispiece]. According to Gordine, she 'had been unhappily married and had fallen into such a state of extreme melancholia and indifference to life that she was being treated in the lunatic asylum'. The first portrait, 'heavy and sombre with sadness', was apparently to arouse the sitter's interest, and she subsequently regained her vitality.[43]

Gordine left Singapore towards the end of May 1935, once she had ensured her works were installed to her satisfaction within the Municipal Buildings. She never returned. Within just seven years, Singapore was under Japanese occupation and the British Empire in Southeast Asia had been swept away.[44] However, the experience of living in that region was central to her subsequent work, her ongoing sense of self-identification and the new home she established in London. As soon as she arrived back in the metropolis from Singapore in July 1935, Gordine initiated divorce proceedings from Dr Garlick on the grounds that he had never consummated their marriage, and embarked upon a new life with Hare. Significantly, the physical environment that she created at Dorich House in her newly built studio-home literally and emotionally embodied her love of Southeast Asia in its architecture, interior design and the treasured objects with which she chose to surround herself.

The strength of Gordine's emotional attachments was evident in later life when she frequently recollected her experiences in her public broadcasts and interviews. In 1950, for example, she told listeners to the BBC Far Eastern Service that in Bali she had been 'carried away' by the beauty of the 'traditional court and peasant dances, still so magically linking daily life with a richer world of

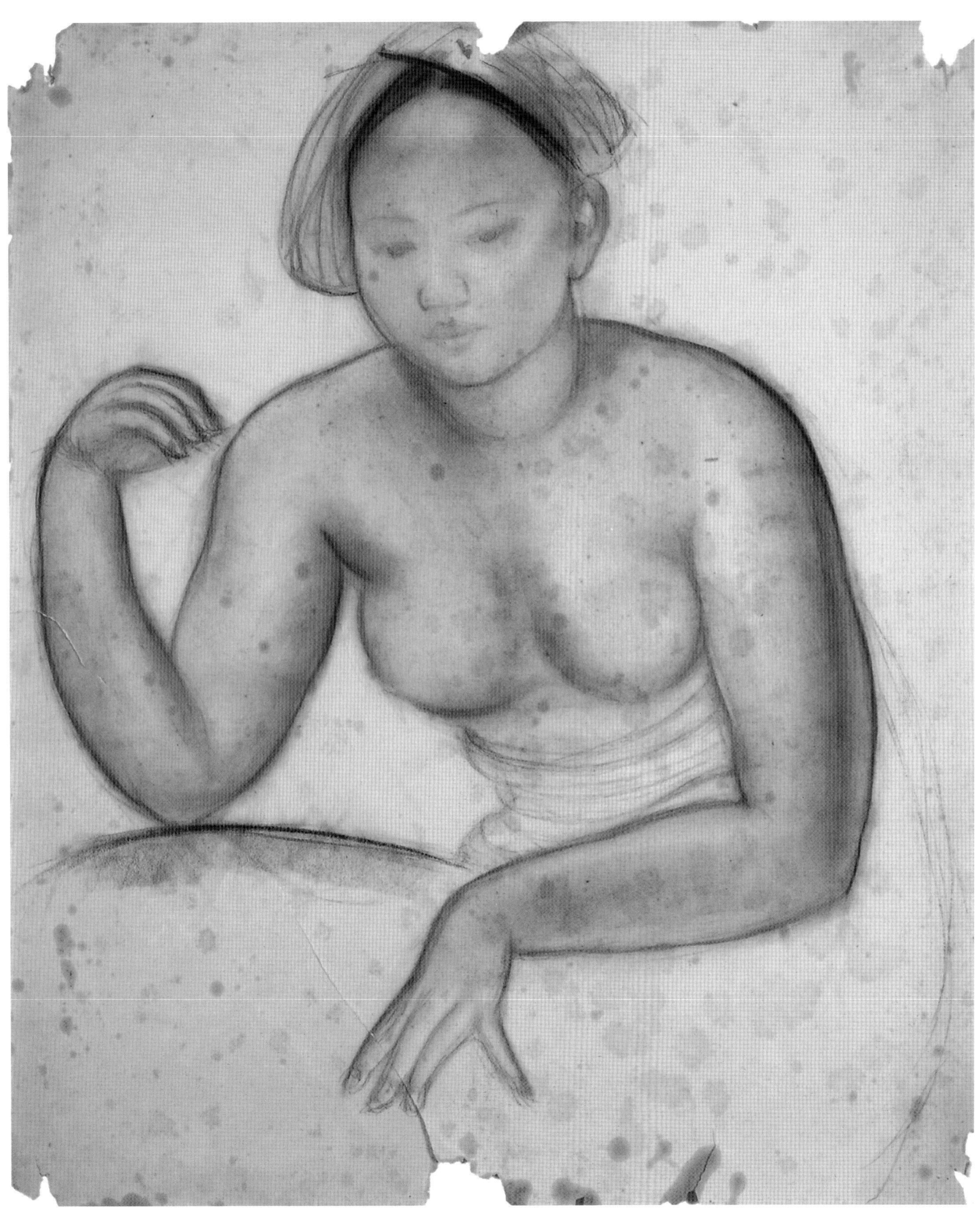

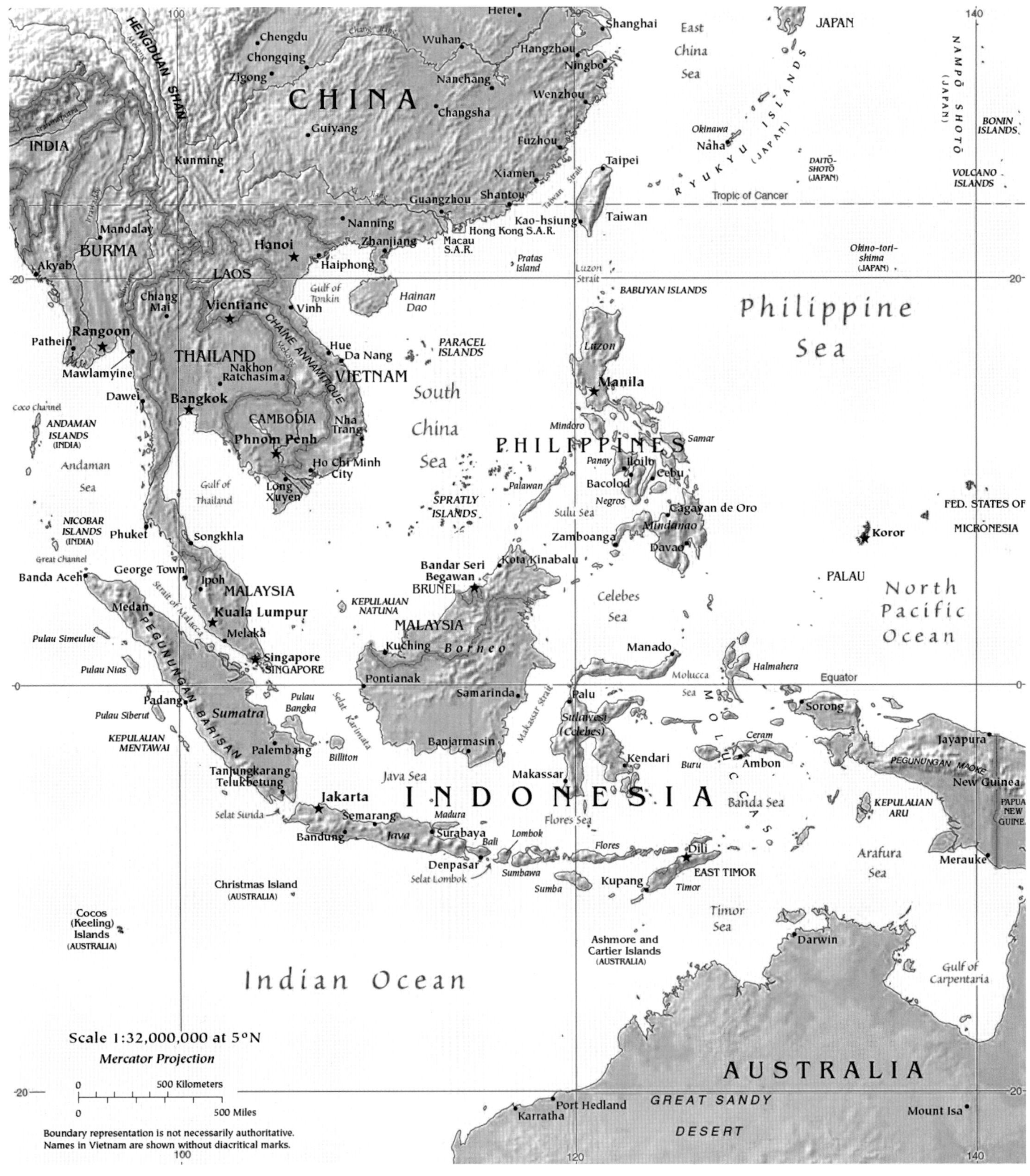

Scale 1:32,000,000 at 5°N

Mercator Projection

0   500 Kilometers

0   500 Miles

Boundary representation is not necessarily authoritative.
Names in Vietnam are shown without diacritical marks.

imagination. When in my home today, I turn on a cherished gramophone record of a gamelan orchestra, I see at once the bamboo groves of southern Bali, where I used to hear at dusk the soft, liquid, rippling music.' [45]

Indeed, later in the same interview, she refers to the 'joy … to bring back to Europe all those living memories of the Far East, after working there for five years', where the 'happy blend of Asia and Europe' sat 'side by side' and paralleled the possibilities of harmonious coexistence.

Gordine's broader knowledge of Asian art was also shared with a range of audiences through the lectures she gave during the war years. The first of these, in December 1940, was delivered to the Royal Asiatic Society, on the subject of 'The Beauty of Asiatic Sculpture',[46] and was published in the *Journal of the Royal Asiatic Society* in January 1941 as the first of a series of eight articles entitled 'Masterpieces of Oriental Art'.

The overall significance of Gordine's work was noted in the *Times* obituary where she was described as 'a sculptress of natural talent who created some of the most spiritual and engaging heads of modern times – particularly from oriental models …' [47] Her drawings in Southeast Asia extend our understanding of this engagement beyond the image of the stereotypical oriental to the entwined histories of empire that open up the interconnected material and imaginary spaces of Europe and its former colonies. Alert to the complexities of gender, class and multiple ethnicities, they are a powerful reminder of the many points of identification that Gordine created and re-created through the intimate and embodied process of drawing.

Southeast Asia and China where Gordine
travelled extensively c. 1930–31 and 1934–35
Image: CIA World Factbook

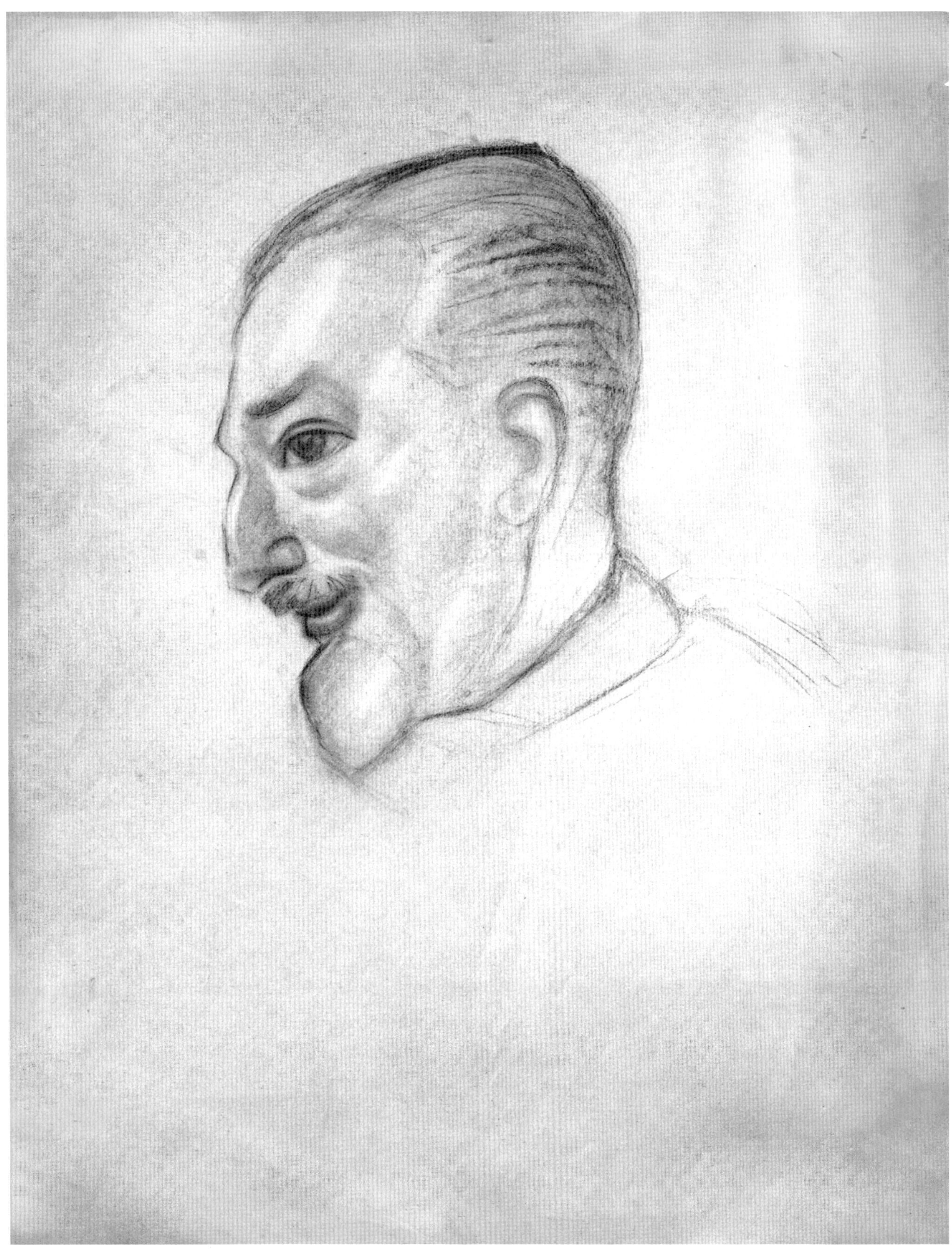

Chapter Three

DRAWING AND PUBLIC COMMISSIONS 1937–64

Jonathan Black

From a relatively early point in her career Gordine expressed a keen interest in producing sculpture for inside, near to, or on the exteriors of public buildings.[1] During her time in Southeast Asia she was particularly impressed by how effectively ancient Khmer and Javanese sculptors had integrated their carvings with surrounding architecture.[2] In 1930 she seized upon an offer, from the Singapore municipal commissioners, to produce bronzes to adorn the interior of the city's recently completed Municipal Buildings.[3] However, an opportunity to provide work for a public space in London did not arise until after she had established herself at Dorich House in the late autumn of 1936 – an unorthodox design which quickly attracted visits from a number of influential individuals. In turn, they quickly became patrons of hers.

Sir Harry Sheil Elster Vanderpant (1866–1955)

The first relevant drawing in this group within the Dorich House Museum collection grew from a somewhat casually issued 'commission' that originated with H.S. Goodhart-Rendel, recently elected president of the Royal Institute of British Architects (RIBA) in London, for Gordine to produce a bronze portrait head of a very important RIBA benefactor, Sir Harry Sheil Elster Vanderpant [Plate 33].

Goodhart-Rendel had first visited Dorich House in July 1937.[4] Three months later he wrote to thank Gordine for her hospitality and to emphasize how impressed he had been by the house. In the letter, almost as an afterthought, he asked Gordine whether she knew of:

Plate 33 Study for the Portrait of Sir Harry Sheil Elster Vanderpant 1937–38
charcoal on paper, 65 x 50 cm
Dorich House Museum

any young sculptor who would not think £100 too low a price for a portrait bust of a benefactor to the Royal Institute of British Architects. This benefactor is middle-aged and, I think a possible, without being an inspiring, subject for a sculptor to tackle. £100 has been allotted by the appropriate committee for obtaining a portrait of him i.e. three dimensions that will look well in the large room that has been chiefly built with his money. The RIBA's idea was to ask the Royal Society of British Sculptors [RBS] for a recommendation, but I feel that to ask a distinguished sculptor personally is likely to obtain for us much better advice   You may imagine the sort of thing that is likely to be produced by a nominee of the Sculptor's Society, and I am very anxious to avoid the disaster of banality into which we might fall. It has occurred to me that you might know of some suitable person who would be glad of the job although I realise that I am being rather a nuisance in bothering you.[5]

Goodhart-Rendel was delighted when, before the week was out, Gordine replied that she would be willing to undertake the commission herself as she was a great admirer of the RIBA and its efforts to improve architectural standards throughout Britain. She also made it clear she was an admirer of Goodhart-Rendel's work and, especially, appreciated his calls for architects to work more closely with sculptors on projects.[6] Ironically, though Goodhart-Rendel was so caustically dismissive of the RBS, Gordine was elected an associate of the society in April 1938. Other sculptors so elected at the same time were Frank Dobson and Eric Gill. This constituted the first sign given to Gordine of serious recognition from a prestigious body within the British art world.[7]

The sitter Goodhart-Rendel had in mind, of course, was the then lord mayor of Westminster, Councillor H.S.E. Vanderpant. In June 1931 he had donated £10,000 to the RIBA New Premises Fund on condition that half should be used to commemorate Mr Henry Louis Florence, vice-president of the RIBA between 1897 and 1899 and later vice-president of the Architect's Benevolent Society. The other half of the donation would be used to fund the 'Henry Louis Florence Travelling Studentship'.[8] Ever since his election to Westminster council, as a Conservative in 1919, Vanderpant had campaigned vigorously to clear slum areas in Pimlico,[9] some of the worst in London, to provide well-designed and hygienic modern housing for working class people, and to greatly increase the provision of maternity care for working class mothers in an effort to reduce Pimlico's dire child mortality rate.[10] All of these causes were dear to 'right-thinking' progressives and the British liberal intelligentsia of the day.[11]

Gordine's bronze head of Vanderpant was unveiled inside the RIBA building on Portland Place early in November 1938. At the ceremony, Goodhart-Rendel lavished praise on Gordine's skill: 'Apart from the great sculptural merit of this bust, there is in it the very remarkable likeness to life … To know Mr Vanderpant is to feel oneself his friend and the bust, with its charming suggestion of modesty and kindliness, is just what his friends would wish it to be.'[12] As for the sitter, he bought a cast of the portrait for himself, which he later left in his will to the Christ's Hospital School for Girls, of which he had been a significant benefactor for many years. For his successful efforts to improve the quality of life for the poorer citizens of Westminster and significantly increase the provision of air raid shelters, Vanderpant was knighted in 1939.[13]

Study in Charcoal related to *Seated Baby*, 1937–38

At the time he was sitting to Gordine, Vanderpant was justly proud of having ensured the creation of the new Westminster City Council Maternity and Child Welfare Centre, opened on Bessborough Gardens, Pimlico, by the Queen in November 1937. According to the *Times*, the new centre would teach 'younger mothers the art of "Mothercraft" – not only the care of the child but also the health of the mother. Two Medical officers will be available to advise mothers on health issues and diet until the children have reached school age.'[14]

Between the wars infant and maternal mortality rates were a cause of concern to many within authority and by 1938 over 3,500 infant welfare clinics had been established by local authorities at the behest of the 1918 Maternity and Child Welfare Act.[15] Many of Gordine's friends were preoccupied with improving child welfare within urban Britain and especially reducing the mortality rate for young working class mothers who tended to have far more children than their middle class counterparts.[16] Lady Ina Cholmondeley, who sat to Gordine for a bronze portrait head in 1937, founded the National Birthday Trust Fund for the Extension of Maternity Services in 1933 with the aim of radically reducing the high level of infant mortality.[17]

Gordine and Vanderpant evidently got on very well indeed, for he soon commissioned a bronze cast of the figure *Seated Baby* she was working on at the time [Plate 34]. Vanderpant wanted the figure to be placed within the entrance area of his new centre in Pimlico. He had already contributed thousands of pounds from his own pocket to make the centre a reality and now paid for the figure to be cast in bronze. *Seated Baby* was formally unveiled by Vanderpant, to much acclaim from guests present at the ceremony, in May 1938.[18]

The sitter for the figure was two-year-old Verena Joan Dawnay, the child of a friend of Richard Hare's sister Patricia. In fact, she was one of the bridesmaids at Patricia's wedding in November 1936 to Charles Milnes-Gaskell.[19] Verena's father was the aristocratic the Hon. Cuthbert Dawnay, owner of West Heslerton Hall near Malton in the East Riding of Yorkshire and a local JP.[20] Intriguingly, in emphasising her plumpness, Gordine has not made Verena appear at all an attractive child. While Gordine never had any children of her own from either of her two marriages, she did enjoy their conversation as well as drawing them.[21] She frequently referred to her own sculptures as her 'children' and expected them to be suitably cherished by their owners.[22]

Study in Charcoal related to *Crowning Glory*, c. 1946

This sensuous drawing [Plate 35] is related to by far one of the most unusual public commissions with which Gordine was involved. She was asked to produce a figure of a nude female playing dreamily with her sensuous long hair. This would, essentially, serve as the new logo for the Eugené Permanent Wave Company which was seeking to promote its unfamiliar haircare product to the cash-strapped British housewife living in the straightened circumstances of Austerity Britain.[23] In the conception of the figure, Gordine looked back to an earlier drawing she had produced c. 1934–35 of a seminaked young woman who had caught her eye in Bali. This drawing led to the bronze figure of *Pagan* first exhibited in the UK at the Leicester Galleries in November 1938. The conception of both *Pagan* and *Crowning Glory* also owes a considerable debt to realisations of the Buddha by the Khmer sculptors at Angkor Wat c. 1181–1215 CE and Buddhist temple carvers at Borobudhur c. 750–830 CE. The pose of the woman in the *Crowning Glory* drawing also strongly suggests that Gordine drew upon the example of many of the illustrations she used for lectures she gave the Royal Asiatic and Royal India Societies, between 1940 and 1944, on the sculpture of ancient India and the civilisations of Southeast Asia.[24]

The relative merits of the 'hot perm' process, championed in the UK by Eugené, as opposed to the 'cold perm' popular in the United States were much debated by British women in the 1940s. In August 1945, for example, a correspondent for Mass Observation noted that two working class housewives on Morecambe beach were engrossed in discussing not the recent dropping of the atomic bomb on Hiroshima but 'the revolutionary new … cold perm' from the United States. Both women bemoaned the fact it would be some time yet before the process would arrive in the UK from the USA.[25]

Apparently, Gordine was delighted with the cast of *Crowning Glory* produced by Morris Singer and with the publicity the figure attracted. In March 1947 she wrote to a friend: 'Yesterday was the unveiling of the *Crowning Glory* in the Savoy [Hotel], terrific success! You would go mad if you saw her in golden bronze against royal blue background. She looked so feminine and serene.'[26] When Maurice Collis, the art critic for the *Observer*, saw the figure on display in the Hall of Beauty at the Ideal Home Exhibition in March 1947, he was impressed: 'It was, then, with surprise that one beheld among contrivances for beautifying

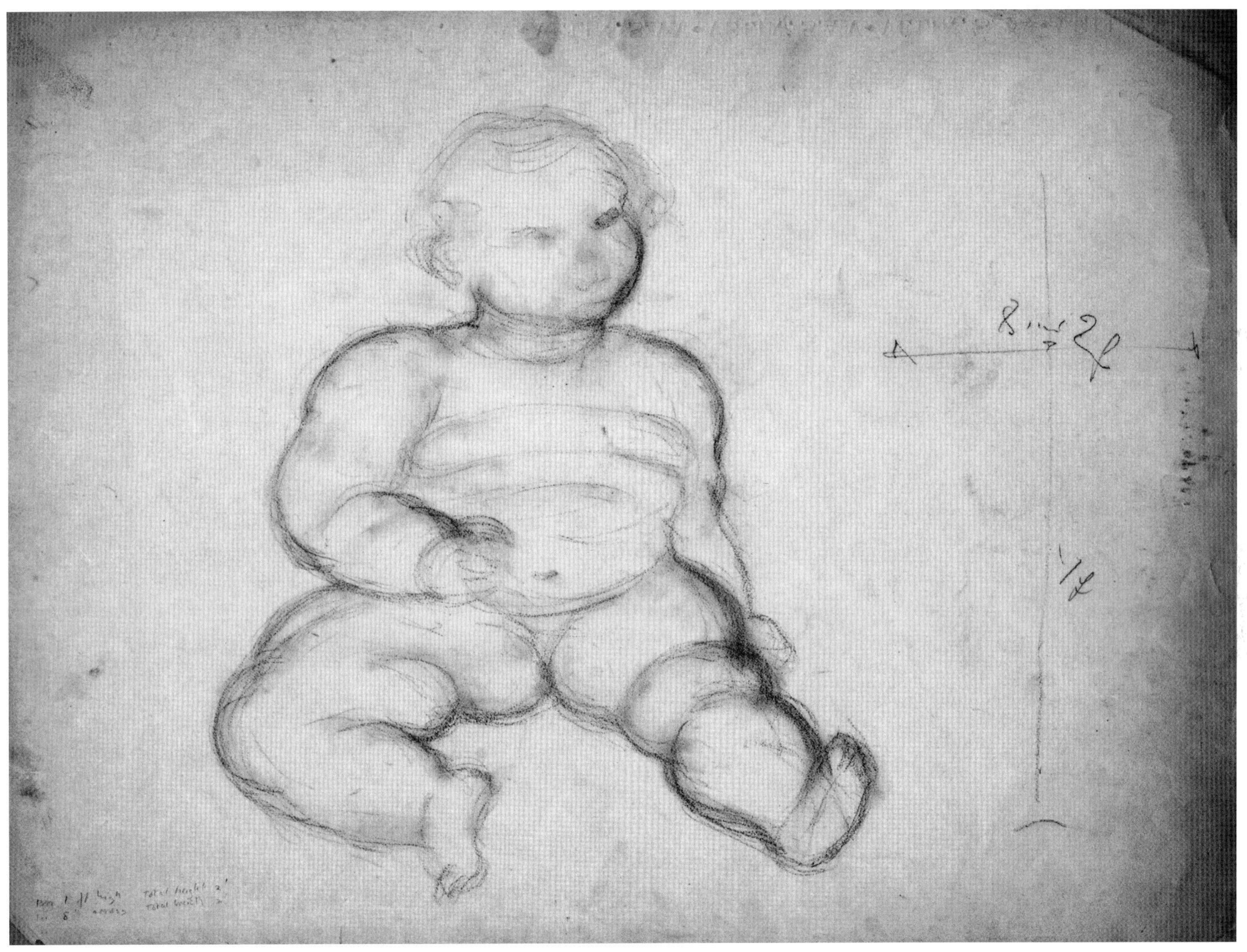

Plate 34 Study of Seated
Baby (Verena Dawnay)
1937–38
charcoal on paper, 50 x 64 cm
Dorich House Museum

the hair, a firm's new mascot, a half-size nude by Dora Gordine, as well modelled a bronze as she has ever done. But good taste is good business, as the directors of this firm know.' [27]

Three charcoal drawings related to the low-relief panel *Power*, 1960

At some seven feet high by five feet wide, this was by far Gordine's largest and most prestigious sculptural commission to date. In May 1960 the Esso petroleum company contacted the Royal Society of Arts in search of 'the names of two or three good sculptors and designers who would be willing to undertake a commission in connection with their new refinery at Milford Haven.' The company was specifically looking for a 'commemorative tablet' to be 'incorporated in the entrance hall of the administrative offices.' [28] By return of post the society's advisor on sculpture, Professor R.Y. Goodden, recommended Gordine, David Wynne and Mark Batten, then president of the RBS. The artists were required to submit a drawing by the middle of July.

Gordine clearly decided from the outset that she would focus on a single figure of a construction worker, seen from behind, stripped to the waist, wearing a safety helmet and helping to guide a steel girder into place. The focus on the impressive musculature of the man's back and on the prominence of his bottom is particularly striking and evident in all three studies [Plates 36–38]. Esso was obviously impressed with the drawing Gordine submitted early in July 1960 for it promptly awarded the commission to her.[29] In a press release, issued to coincide with the eventual unveiling ceremony, Esso declared that the artist's 'sense of pure form in sculpture, heedless alike of straight realism and exaggerated abstraction, and the delicacy of her modelling combine to give her bronzes tremendous power … we venture to suggest, this plaque is a striking example of her work.' [30]

As so often in examples of her past work, such as figures in bronze of female ballet dancers from the late 1940s like *Berceuse* (1946–47) and *Demi-Plié* (1948–49) and a series of drawings of flamenco dancers from 1954–55 [Plate 39], Gordine was preoccupied with depicting well-developed, disciplined musculature and with the human body under strain and in movement. In this particular case, the design is dominated by the body as a locus of power and energy rather than on the contribution made by machinery and technology. For Gordine, it was the people building the refinery, rather than the refinery itself, which should be the real focus for attention. Later in 1960, she explained to Esso that the panel, to which she gave the title *Power*, had been inspired by 'the idea of oil as a great modern source of power, fluidity and movement … linked with the human form, with human beings whose needs are being served by this refinement of crude energy. It is a tribute to the men who built and to those who will operate the company's refinery at Milford Haven.' [31]

Plate 35 Study for Crowning Glory 1946
charcoal on paper, 49 x 63 cm
Dorich House Museum

overleaf, left
Plate 36 Preparatory Study for the Bronze Low-Relief Power 1960
charcoal on paper, 65 x 50.3 cm
Dorich House Museum

overleaf, right
Plate 37 Preparatory Study for the Bronze Low-Relief Power 1960
charcoal on paper, 65 x 50.3 cm
Dorich House Museum

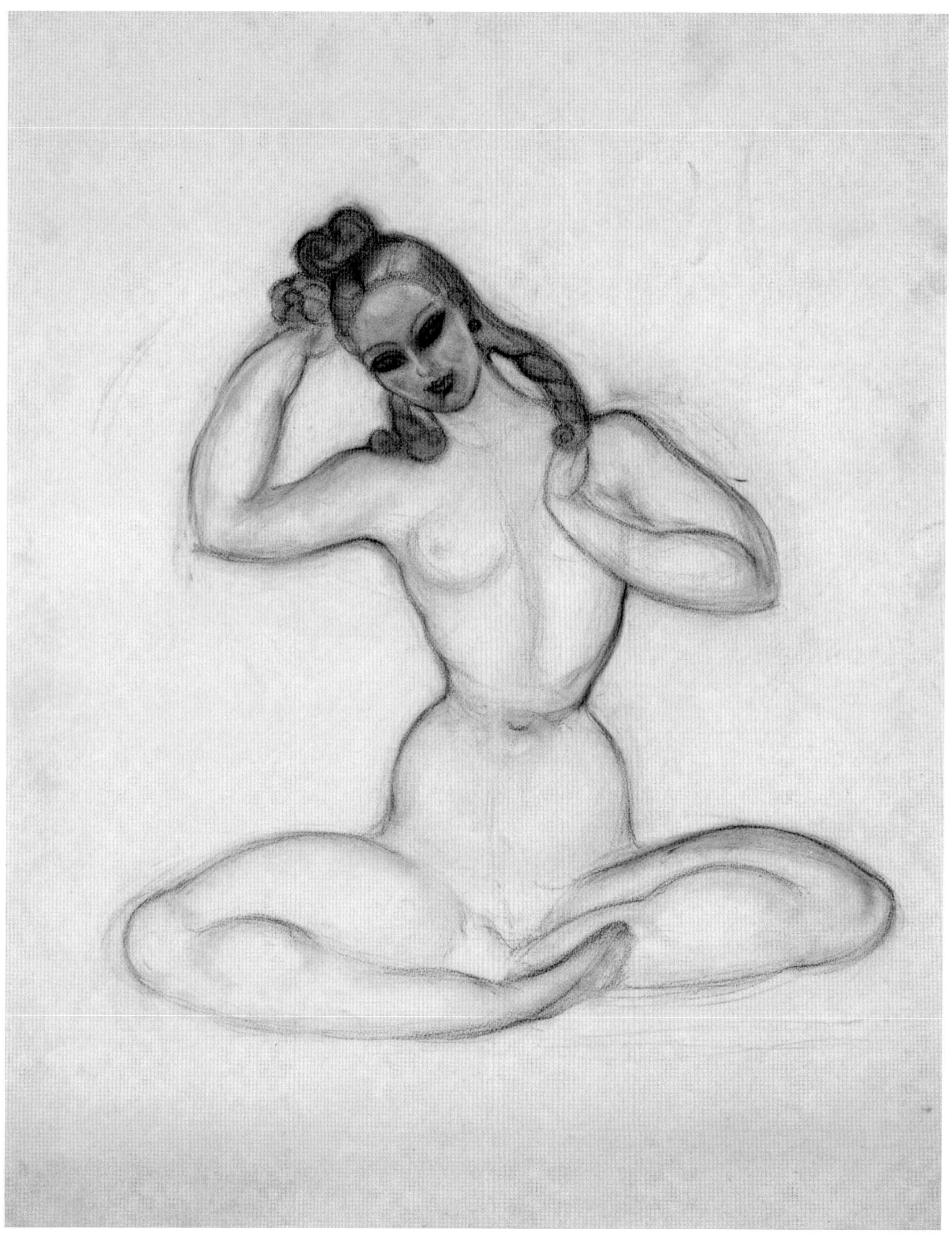

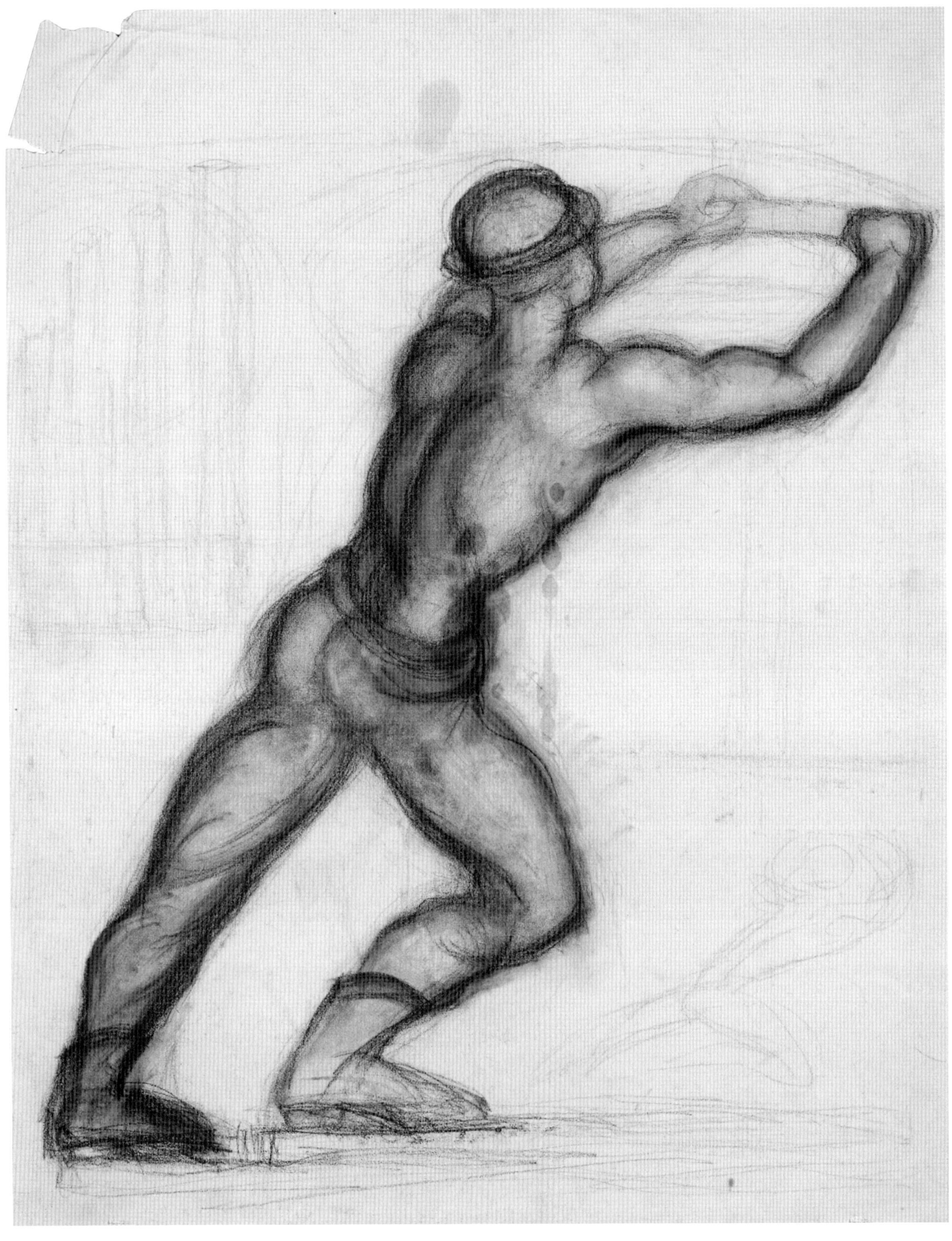

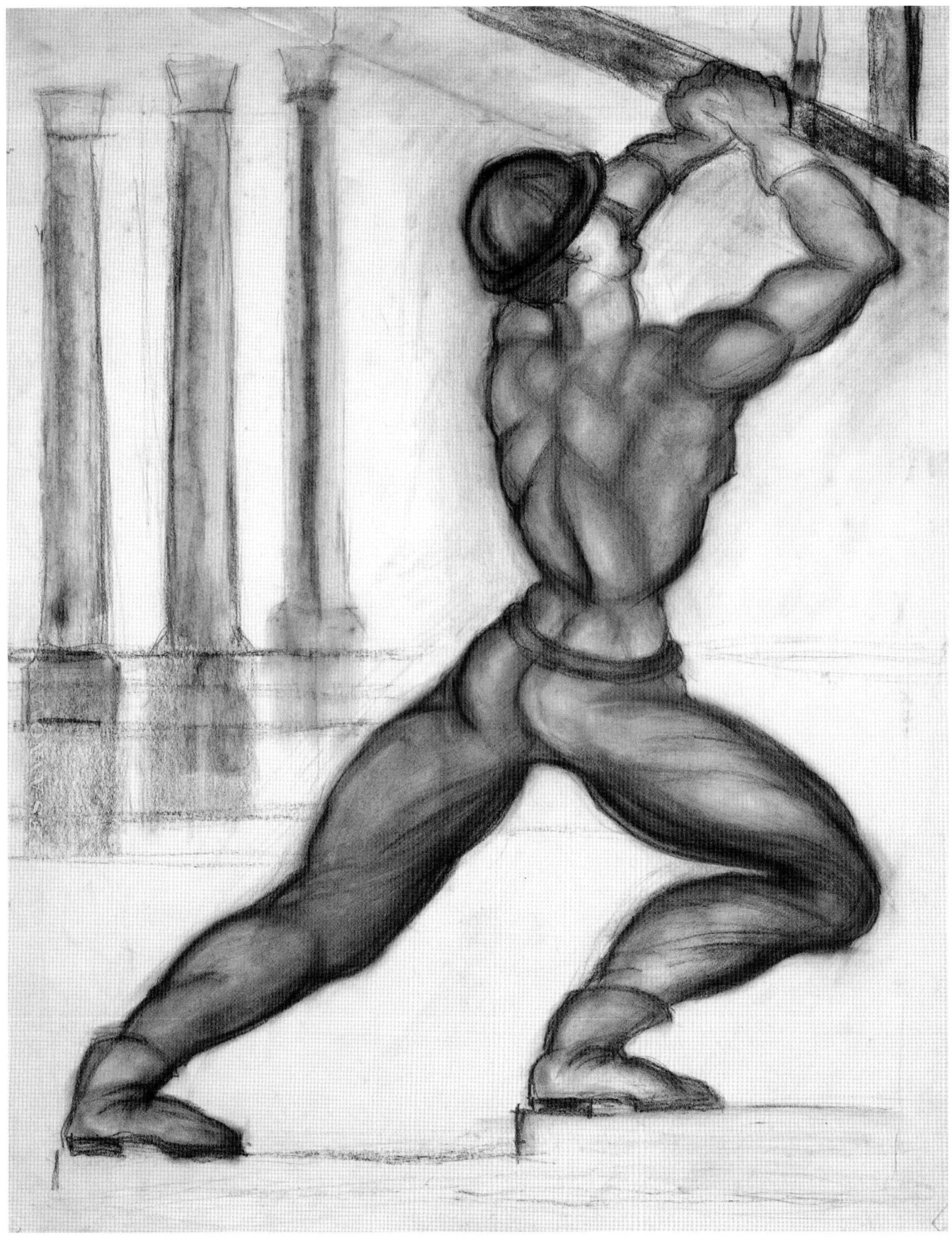

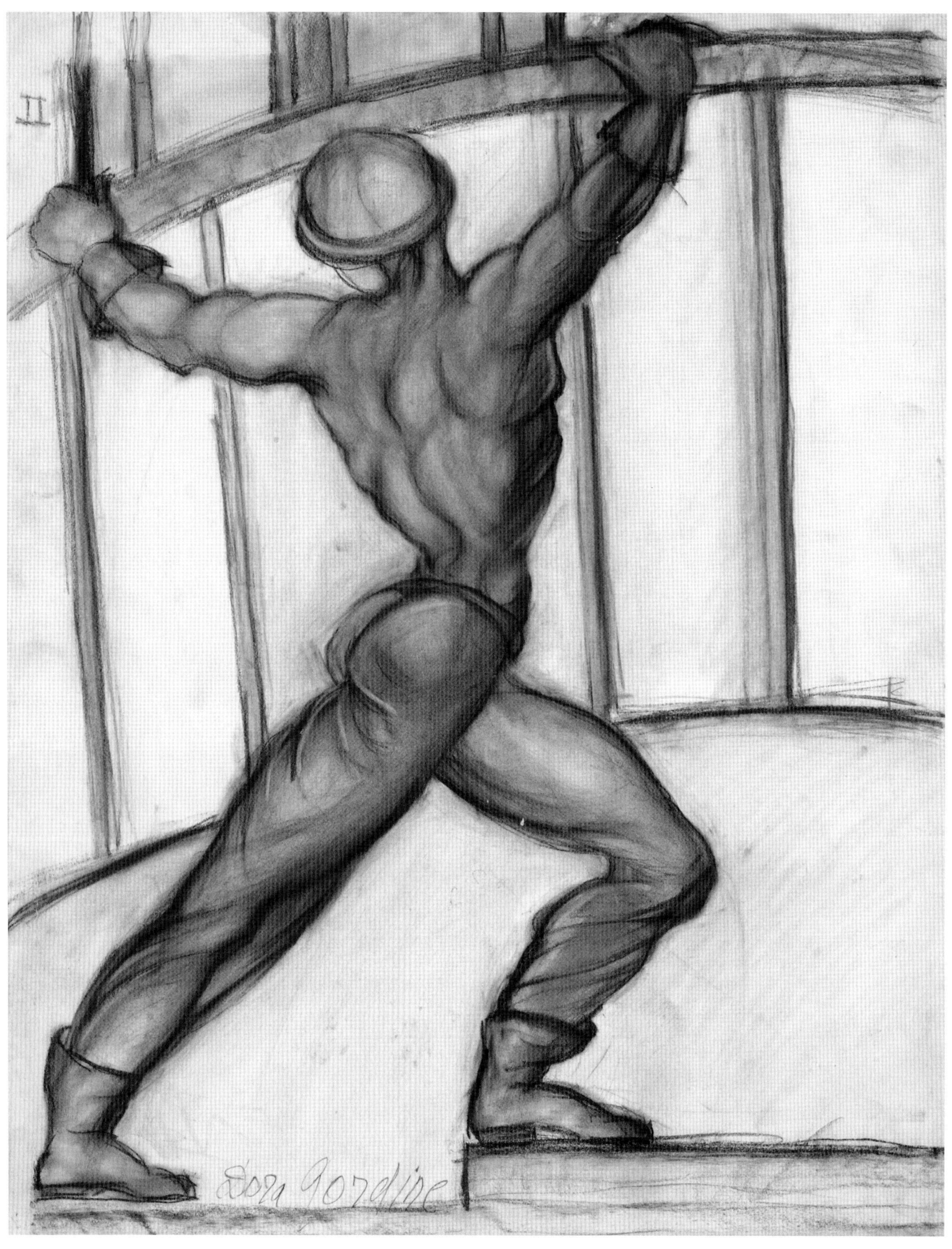
II
Dora Gordine

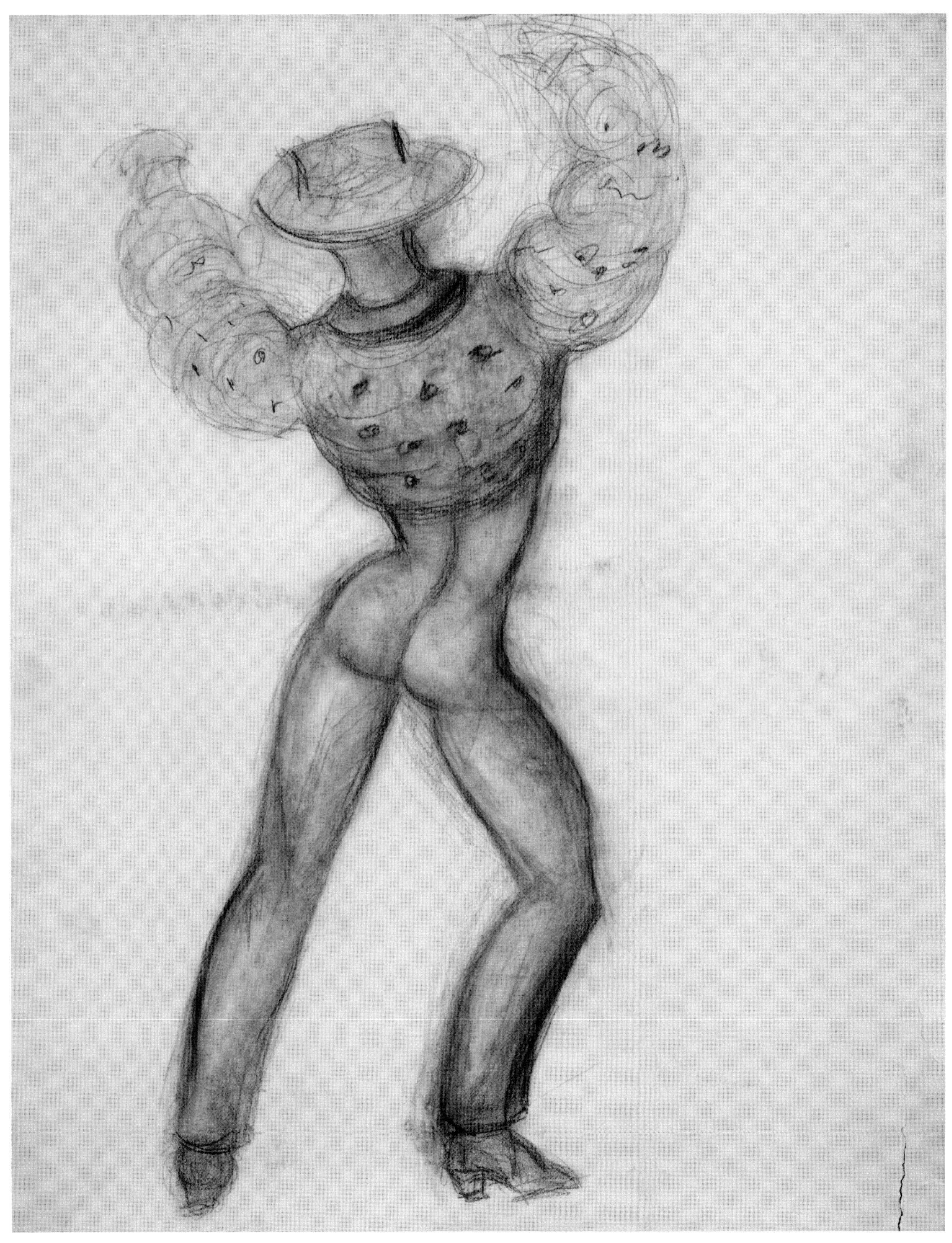

The figure Gordine conceived owes a considerable debt to the heroically striving Stakhanovite worker depicted, in a suitably noble Socialist Realist manner, everywhere in public spaces throughout the Soviet Union from the mid-1930s until well into the 1970s. Richard Hare doubtless saw numerous examples during a trip he made to Moscow and Leningrad between March and August 1945 as part of his duties at the Ministry of Information. Indeed, it may not be entirely coincidental that in his 1947 book *Russian Literature: From Pushkin to the Present Day* Richard Hare discussed a Soviet writer called Fyodor Vasilievich Gladkov (1883–1958) and his 1928 book in praise of the First Soviet Five Year Plan, *Power*. However, her charcoal designs are invigorated by an energy and dynamism less evident in the final bronze that recall the bold figure drawings of Expressionists such as Käthe Kollwitz and Max Beckmann she encountered in late 1920s Berlin.

The title may well have also had an additional, topical, meaning: the production, pricing and distribution of oil conferred a very real degree of 'power' in the world by the end of the '50s. The bulk of the world's oil was extracted in the Middle East where the USA, after the Suez debacle of 1956, had recently supplanted Great Britain as the dominant influence. Earlier in the decade the US and UK secret services had collaborated to engineer continued Western control over Iranian oil by overthrowing the Iranian nationalist leader Mohammed Mossadeq in August 1953.[32]

The relief was unveiled by the Duke of Edinburgh on 3 November 1960. Gordine met him but was not left with a favourable impression.[33] Proud of her achievement, Gordine's husband specially sent a photograph of *Power* to a mutual friend of theirs, who was in charge of public relations at the Indianapolis Museum of Art. Richard Hare described the work as 'a magnificent bronze bas-relief.' He presumably thought that, if the photograph was well received, it might result in a commission for his wife.[34]

A few months later, the *Connoisseur* magazine echoed Hare's comment on *Power*, declaring that the 'bronze relief executed by Dora Gordine, the internationally-known sculptress [has been] executed with outstanding power and imagination …'[35]

Three charcoal drawings related to the bronze figure group *Mother and Child*, 1962–63

At just under four feet high and eight feet long, *Mother and Child* was the largest and most ambitious piece of sculpture Gordine ever made. It was also her last major piece of work. The three preparatory drawings which have survived [Plates 40–42] suggest that Gordine, once she had arrived at a composition comprising two figures, thought long and hard as to how they should interact, balancing

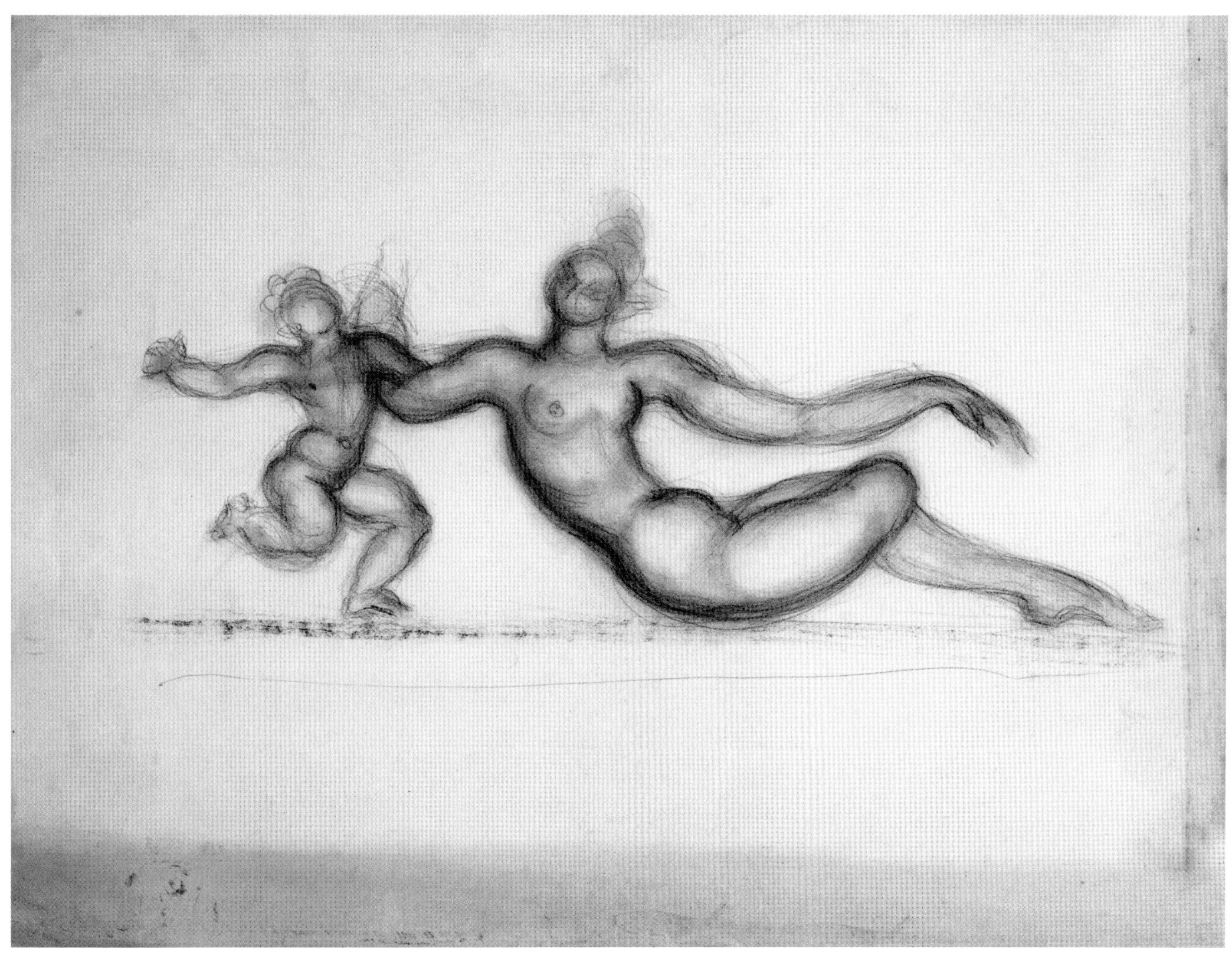

Plate 40 Preparatory Study
for the Bronze Figure Group
Mother and Child 1962
charcoal on paper, 49 x 63.4 cm
Dorich House Museum

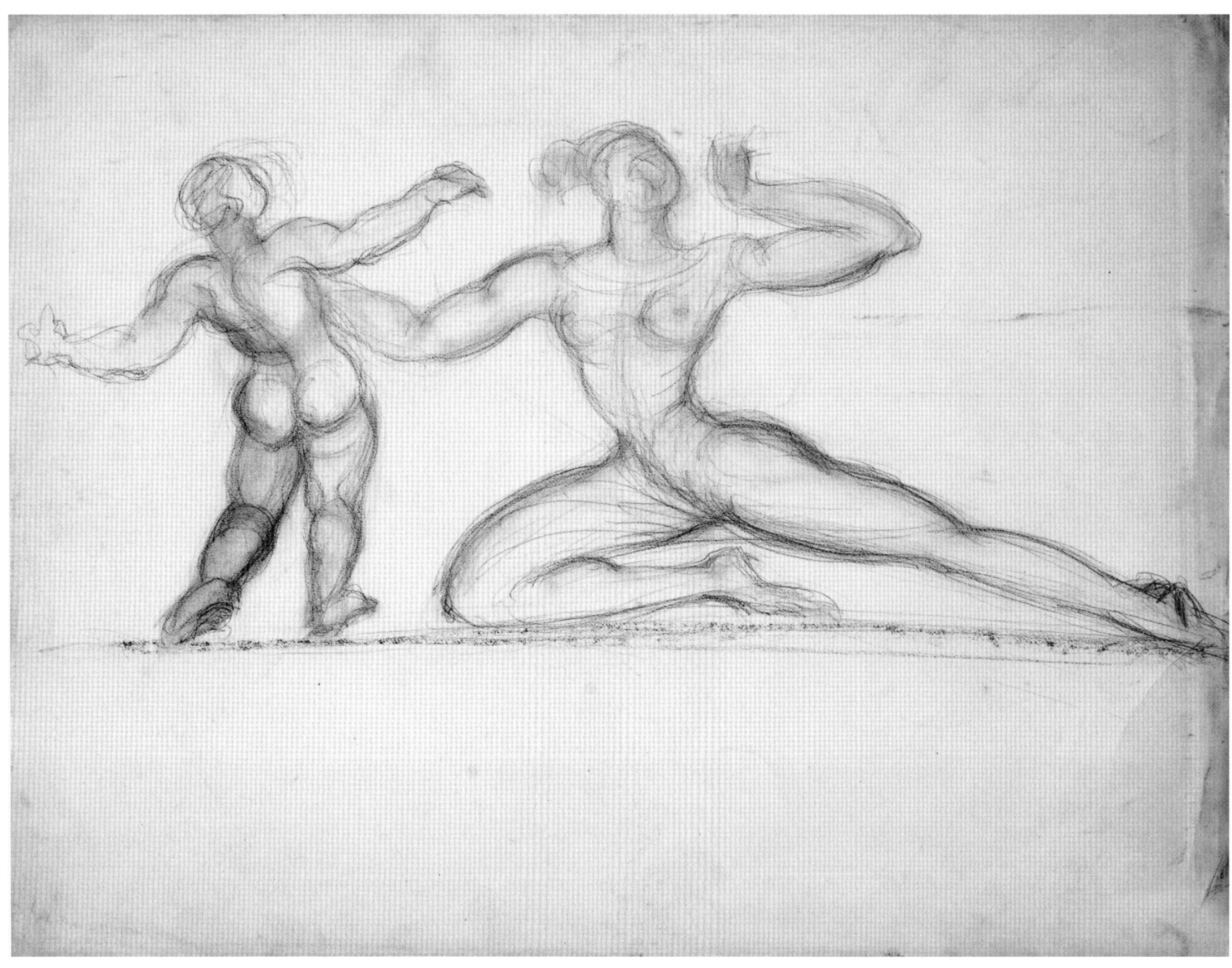

Plate 41 Preparatory Study
for the Bronze Figure Group
Mother and Child 1962
charcoal on paper, 49 x 63.4 cm
Dorich House Museum

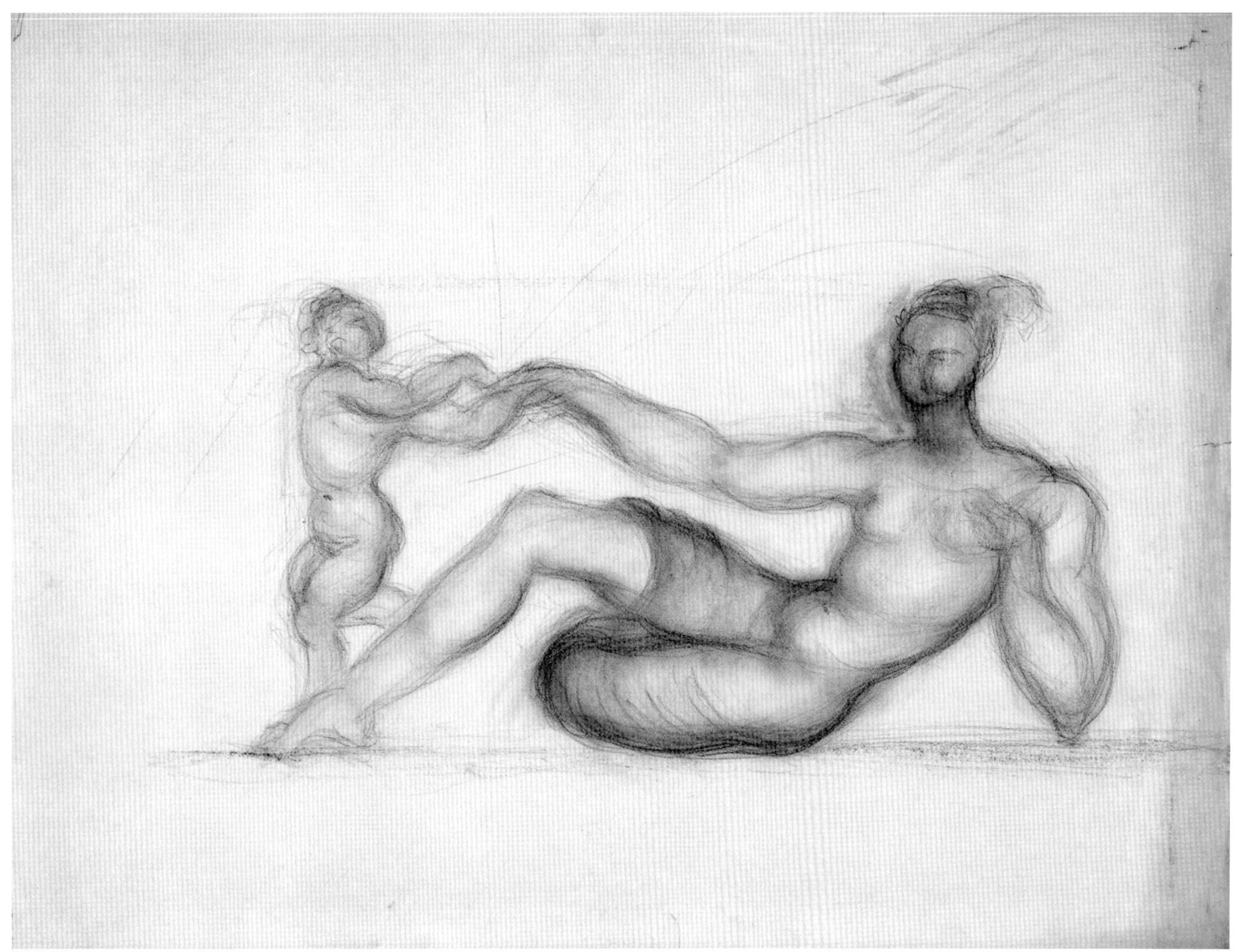

Plate 42 Preparatory Study
for the Bronze Figure Group
Mother and Child 1962
charcoal on paper, 49 x 63.4 cm
Dorich House Museum

the mother as a strong reclining horizontal with the male child standing as an eye-catching and energetic vertical presence. For the conception of the female figure Gordine appears to have harked back to the impressively weighty reclining female nudes Maillol produced during the 1920s for out-of-door settings such as his *Monument to Cezanne* and *La Mediterranée*. Casts of both were installed in the Tuileries Gardens in 1929 by the French state and it is highly likely Gordine was aware of them during the time she spent in Paris in the 1930s. She is known to have visited the Maillol retrospective held in the Petit Palais in May 1937 – part of the Paris Exposition Universelle – where Gordine would have seen his recently finished recumbent female nude *The Mountain* on display. The significant impact of Maillol's example on Gordine's approach to figuration was noted by many observers throughout her career.[36]

Mother and Child was commissioned in 1962 for the entrance area of the new Royal Marsden Cancer Hospital at Sutton, Surrey, by Professor Sir David Smithers (1908–95), the charismatic and pioneering radiologist who was the hospital's first director between 1963 and 1973. The bronze was unveiled by Queen Elizabeth II in May 1963 and Gordine provided the inscription on the plinth which reads: 'This Mother and Child is a symbol of love and confidence, health, protection and happiness, set here to express our purpose to welcome, comfort, relieve and cure.' [37] The inscription very much reflects Professor Smithers's strongly held belief that the health of his cancer patients could be significantly affected, for good or ill, by the emotional state of the patient's nearest and dearest. Indeed, he became convinced that if the patient was in a positive state of mind this actually enhanced the beneficial impact of chemotherapy sessions.[38]

The series of drawings related to *Mother and Child* demonstrates convincingly that Gordine was still more than capable of producing graphic work up to the highest standards, imbued with those qualities of power and strength tempered by delicacy and subtlety that observers had praised throughout her richly accomplished career.

NOTES

INTRODUCTION

1 Marie Dormoy, 'Dora Gordine: Sculpteur', *L'Amour de l'Art*, May 1927, p.166.

2 Twenty-four page Spirabloc, Croquis Design, Paris, including loose leaf drawings from Paris and Berlin, Dorich House Collection.

3 Gordine's passion for the subject is evident in one of her first published interviews: 'Sculpture in Attap Studio. Miss Dora Gordine', *Straits Times of Singapore*, 12 August 1930, p.14.

4 Gordine's respect for Maillol was first mentioned by Dormoy in 'Dora Gordine: Sculpteur', *L'Amour de l'Art*, May 1927, p.166. Two years later, she referred to Maillol as her 'God', *Dörfische Zeitung*, Berlin, 23 September 1929, clipping, Archives, Dorich House Museum (henceforth DHM).

5 'Sculpture in an Attap Studio. Miss Dora Gordine', *Straits Times of Singapore*, 12 August 1930, p.14.

6 Gordine hinted at respect for Despiau and Bernard in Gerald Reitlinger, 'Paris Notes: Dora Gordine', *Drawing and Design*, February 1928, p.59.

7 Frank Rutter, 'Around the Galleries', *Sunday Times*, 9 July 1933, p.7.

8 Gordine was first mentioned in connection with Dobson by R.H. Wilenski, 'Girl Sculptor Genius', *Evening Standard*, 5 October 1928, clipping Archives, DHM.

9 Eric Kennington met Gordine in London c. October 1928 and, unsuccessfully, attempted to persuade her to take up stone carving.

10 In 1929 Wilenski mentioned Gordine's work in relation to contributions by Moore and Dobson to an exhibition held at the Sydney Burney Gallery in London. R.H. Wilenski, 'Modern and African Sculpture', *Observer*, 25 November 1929, p.15.

11 Arthur Symons, 'Sculpture: Dora Gordine', *Spectator*, 4 November 1938, p.768.

12 R.P. Bedford (Curator of Modern Drawings) to Sir Eric Maclagen, 8 November 1938, Archives, Victoria & Albert Museum, London (henceforth: V&A).

13 Sir Eric Maclagen to Dora Gordine, 9 November 1938, Archives, V&A.

14 Lord Ivor, for example, was one of Britain's leading interwar collectors of sculpture and drawings by Maillol, Despiau, Dobson and Epstein. 'Lord Ivor Churchill. Obituary', *Times*, 18 September 1956, p.11.

15 Sir Eric Maclagen to Dora Gordine, 22 December 1938, Archives, V&A.

CHAPTER ONE

1 Jonathan Black, 'Portraiture, Patronage and Networking', in Jonathan Black and Brenda Martin, *Dora Gordine: Sculptor, Artist, Designer* (London: Philip Wilson, 2007), Chapter One.

2 Noel Annan, *Our Age: Portrait of a Generation* (London: Weidenfeld & Nicolson, 1990), p.3.

3 Annan, 1990, pp.72–73.

4 Martin Pugh, *We Danced All Night: A Social History of Britain Between The Wars* (London: The Bodley Head, 2008), pp.97–98.

5 Eric Newton, 'Around the Galleries', *Sunday Times*, 6 November 1938, p.5.

6 The term 'public relations' was only just then entering general parlance in the United Kingdom – imported from the United States during the late 1920s. Cathy Ross, *Twenties London: A City in the Jazz Age* (London: Philip Wilson Publishers, 2003), pp.48–50.

7 Sir Alec Martin to D.S. MacColl, 18 October 1937, MacColl Papers, Archives, Glasgow University [henceforth: AGU].

8 Black and Martin, London, 2007, pp.239–40.

9 Richard Hare to D.S. MacColl, 26 April 1938, MacColl Papers, AGU.

10 Dora Gordine to D.S. MacColl, 29 April 1938, MacColl Papers, AGU.

11 'The Vanishing Moustache', *Daily Telegraph*, 28 October 1938, Clipping, Archives, DHM.

12 Dora Gordine to D.S. MacColl, early October 1938, MacColl Papers, AGU.

13 H.S. Goodhart-Rendel to Charles Holden, 13 December 1938, London University Archives, Senate House Library, London.

14 Black and Martin, London, 2007, pp.51–52.

15 Black and Martin, London, 2007, p.239.

16 *Daily Express*, 6 October 1938, p.3.

17 *Queen*, 10 November 1938, clipping, Archives, DHM.

18 Black and Martin, London, 2007, p.239.

19 *Times*, 14 January 1939, p.10.

20 Eric Newton wrote that the head was 'splendidly modelled', *Sunday Times*, 6 November 1938, p.5.

21 David Kynaston, *Austerity Britain: 1945–51* (London: Bloomsbury, 2007), p.218.

22 Alan Bennett, *Untold Stories* (London: Faber & Faber, 2005), p.299.

23 Godfrey Winn, *The Infirm Glory: An Autobiography* (London: Michael Joseph, 1967), p.368.

24 *Straits Times of Singapore*, 7 May 1935, p.13.

25 W. Somerset Maugham to Kate Bruce, 23 January 1952, Maugham Papers, Berg Collection, New York Public Library.

26 Jane Fletcher Geniesse, *Freya Stark: Passionate Nomad* (London: Chatto & Windus, 1999), p.141.

27 Ibid., p.184.

28 Entry for 5 November 1938, Diaries of Sir Sydney Cockerell, British Library, London (henceforth: BLL).

29 *Times*, 5 December 1938, p.15.

30 The dinner was held on the 15 December 1938. Stark Papers, Harry Ransom Humanities Research Centre, University of Texas at Austin.

31 Entry for 26 December 1938, Cockerell Diaries, BLL.

32 Geniesse, 1999, p.237.

33 Dora Gordine to Sir Sydney Cockerell, 20 February 1939, Cockerell Papers, BLL.

34 Geniesse, 1999, pp.29–30.

35 Ibid., p.158.

36 Ibid., p.160.

37 In January 1945, for example, Gordine attended a lunch given to celebrate Stark's recent successful tour of the Middle East. Entry for 15 January 1945, Cockerell Diaries, BLL.

38 Freya Stark, *The Coast of Incense: Autobiography 1933–1939* (London: John Murray, 1953), p.238.

39 Dora Gordine to Sir Sydney Cockerell, 26 September 1939, Cockerell Papers, BLL.

40 The Anglo-Soviet Relations Section was established in October 1941; it was expanded to Divisional status in March 1942 – around the time that Richard Hare was assigned to it. INF/1/147, National Archives, Kew, London.

41 Dora Gordine to Sir Sydney Cockerell, 27 December 1942, Cockerell Papers, BLL.

42 Entry for 7 June 1944, Cockerell Diaries, BLL. Sir Sydney noted meeting Gordine with Lady Leconfield at an exhibition of 'Indian Art' at the Victoria & Albert Museum mounted by the Royal India Society.

43 *Times*, 22 May 1936, p.11.

44 Sir Eric Maclagen to Dora Gordine, 9 November 1938, Maclagan Papers, Archives, V&A.

45 *Times*, 5 December 1938, p.15.

46 Entry for 16 June 1944, Cockerell Diaries, BLL.

47 Dora Gordine to Sir Sydney Cockerell, 7 October 1945, Cockerell Papers, BLL.

48 Entry for 19 December 1944, Cockerell Diaries, BLL.

49 Dora Gordine to Sir Sydney Cockerell, 12 July 1943, Cockerell Papers, BLL.

50 *Daily Telegraph*, 6 November 1964, clipping, Archives, DHM.

51 *Chicago Herald Tribune*, 3 December 1939, clipping, Archives, DHM.

52 Ysenda Maxtone-Graham, *The Real Mrs Miniver: The Life of Jan Struther* (London: History Press, 2007).

53 *Daily Telegraph*, 5 November 1964, clipping, Archives, DHM.

54 Interview with Mrs Patricia Bates, 22 February 2005, transcript, Archives, DHM.

55 *Times*, 7 November 1942, p.2.

56 Rodric Braithwaite, *Moscow 1941: A City and Its People at War* (London: Profile Books, 2006), p.111.

57 *Times*, 25 November 1942, p.6.

58 Gordine gave a 'presentation' of her recent war drawings, which may well have included the portrait of Pavlichenko, to the War Artists Advisory Committee [WAAC] on 25 November 1942. However, although the WAAC expressed polite interest in Gordine's work, it did not offer her an official commission. Minutes of the WAAC, 25 November 1942, GP/72/G, Department of Art, Imperial War Museum, London.

59 Dora Gordine to Sir Sydney Cockerell, 27 December 1942, Cockerell Papers, BLL.

60 Professor Christopher Andrew revealed that Smolka/Smollett was a Soviet spy, codenamed 'Abo', in 1999. Peter Davison, ed., *Orwell and Politics* (London: Penguin, 2001), p.228.

61 Ibid., p.507.

62 Mati Laur, ed., *The History of Estonia* (Tallinn: AS BIT, 2002), p.267.

63 Mark Rybak (Curator of the Tallinn Jewish Museum) to Dr Jonathan Black, 3 March 2008, Archives, DHM.

64 Lauer, 2002, p.275.

65 Nikolai was shot in the courtyard of Tallinn's central prison on 6 October 1941. Mark Rybak to Dr Jonathan Black, 25 February 2008, Archives, DHM.

66 *Daily Telegraph*, 22 July 1943, clipping, Archives, DHM.

67 Juliet Gardiner, *Wartime: 1939–1945* (London: Review, 2005), pp.224–25.

68 George Orwell, 'The Lion and the Unicorn: Part 1', Bernard Crick, ed., *George Orwell Essays* (London: Penguin, 2000), pp.141–43.

69 Gardiner, 2005, p.125.

70 Gardiner, 2005, p.72.

71 Dora Gordine to Sir Sydney Cockerell, 12 July 1943, Cockerell Papers, BLL.

72 George Orwell, 'As I Please', *Tribune*, 18 February 1944 in Peter Davison, ed., *Orwell in Tribune. As I Please and other Writings, 1943–47* (London: Politicos, 2006), p.101.

73 Dora Gordine to Sir Sydney Cockerell, 2 August 1943, Cockerell Papers, BLL.

74 Black and Martin, London, 2007, p.58.

75 Obituary of Lady Elsie Goold-Adams, The *Times*, 28 August 1952, p.1.

76 Entry for 19 September 1944, Diaries of Elizabeth Main, née Goold-Adams, transcript, Archives, DHM.

77 *Times*, 30 October 1941, p.7. As it happened, Gordine had known Lady Isobel Cripps since the late 1920s.

78 *Scotsman*, 20 April 1946, p.4.

79 Black and Martin, London, 2007, pp.246–47.

80 Entry for 18 November 1944, Diaries of Elizabeth Main, née Goold-Adams, transcript, DHM.

81 Dora Gordine to Muriel Orr-Ewing, undated (c. October 1949), Special Collections, University Archives, University of New York at Buffalo.

82 Entry for 11 January 1945, Diaries of Elizabeth Main, née Goold-Adams, transcript, DHM.

83 *Daily Telegraph*, 19 October 1945, clipping, Archives, DHM.

84 *Times*, 10 March 1938, p.6.

85 Frank Roberts, *Dealing with Dictators: The Destruction and Revival of Europe, 1930–1970* (London: Weidenfeld & Nicolson, 1991), p.16.

86 Entry for 20 January 1945, Diaries of Elizabeth Main, née Goold-Adams, transcript, DHM.

87 *Times*, 22 December 1945, p.4.

88 *Times*, 1 July 1947, p.4.

89 *Times*, 4 November 1948, p.3.

90 *Evening Standard*, 26 October 1949, clipping, Archives, DHM. In 1947 Gordine asked Sheikh Wahba whether he would sit to her, but he declined. He did allow, however, his beautiful Paris-educated wife to sit for a bronze portrait head. This was exhibited as *Arabian Princess* at the Leicester Galleries in 1949.

91 *Times*, 28 December 1951, p.4.

92 *Times*, 6 August 1952, p.4.

93 Annan, 1990, p.222.

94 Roberts, 1991, p.186. Sir Frank's Lebanese-born wife, Celeste (Cella), sat to Gordine for a bronze portrait head in the mid 1950s.

95 Diana White to Esther Pissarro, 2 November 1928, Pissarro Papers, Ashmolean Museum, Oxford [henceforth: AMO].

96 Orovida Pissarro to Margaret Pilkington, c. June 1939, Pissarro Papers, AMO.

97 Dora Gordine to Orovida Pissarro, undated (c. June 1956), Pissarro Papers, AMO.

98 Orovida Pissarro to Ian Roberston (Keeper of Western Art), c. July 1957, Pissarro Papers, AMO.

99 John Drummond, *Speaking of Diaghilev* (London: Faber & Faber, 1998), p.55.

100 Biographical Information, Archives, Royal Asiatic Society [RAS], London.

101 Entry for 14 June 1962, Proceedings of the Council of the Royal Asiatic Society, Archives, RAS.

102 *Times*, 10 January 1963, p.11.

103 *Times*, 24 October 1962, p.11.

104 Annan, 1990, p.178.

105 Black and Martin, 2007, p.202.

CHAPTER TWO

1 Letter of Richard Hare to D.S. MacColl, 31 May 1938, MacColl Papers, Archives, Glasgow University.

2 Dora Gordine 'Beauty in the Home', *Not Only For Women*, BBC Far Eastern Service Radio, 18 April 1950, BBC Written Archives, Reading.

3 Gordine knew several male artists in the late 1920s who had visited or planned to visit Southeast Asia, including C.R.W. Nevinson whom she had exhibited alongside at the Leicester Galleries in October 1928, his close friend the concert pianist Mark Hambourg (1879–1960), and the German cubist painter Fritz Kronenberg (1901–60) with whom she had exhibited at the Galerie Flechtheim in Berlin in September 1929, and may have known from her Paris days. See Jonathan Black, 'An Unsettling Aura of Inscrutability: Imperialism, Racial Stereotyping and the Construction of the 'Exotic' by British Women Sculptors Between the Wars' from *Agency and Mediation: Women's Contribution to Visual Culture Between the Wars, 1918–1939*, ed. Karen Brown, (Aldershot: Ashgate, 2008).

4 See, for example, Susan Hillier (ed.), *The Myth of Primitivism* (London and New York: Routledge, 1991); Edward Said, Orientalism (London and New York: Routledge, 2003), and Reina Lewis, *Rethinking Orientalism: Women, Travel and the Ottoman Harem* (London: I.B. Tauris, New York: Rutgers, 2004).

5 A number of contemporary British female sculptors such as Hazel Armour (whom Gordine had first met in Paris early in 1925), Elsa Fraenkel (whom Gordine knew by 1929) and Dora Clarke seized the opportunity during the latter half of the 1920s to visit British colonial possessions in East and South Africa to produce 'ethnic heads'. See Black, 'An Unsettling Aura of Inscrutability'.

6 Black, 'Portraiture, Patronage and Networking', in *Dora Gordine: Sculptor, Artist, Designer,* Black and Martin (London: Philip Wilson, 2007), Chapter One.

7 Gerald Reitlinger, 'Dora Gordine', *Drawing and Design*, February 1928, p.59.

8 Lucian Cordier, 'Pointes Sèches', *La Rumeur*, July 1928, clipping, Archives, Dorich House Museum, London.

9 Margaret Shennan, *Out in the Midday Sun: The British in Malaya 1880–1960* (London: John Murray, 2004), pp.182–84.

10 *Straits Times of Singapore*, 21 July 1931, p.18.

11 Charles Allen, *Tales from the South China Seas,* (London: Abacus, 2001), pp.47–49.

12 Shennan, 2004, p.148.

13 John Keay, *Last Post: The End of Empire in the Far East* (London: John Murray, 2005), pp.134–35.

14 The population of the state was just over half a million of which there were: 235,000 Malays, 214,000 Chinese, 51,000 Indians and only 719 Europeans. *Straits Times*, 21 July 1931, p.18.

15 See Roland Braddell, *The Lights of Singapore* (London: Methuen, 1934), p.107.

16 Shennan, 2004, p.54.

17 *Straits Times,* 16 September 1930, p.22.

18 P.G. Konody, *Observer,* 7 October 1928, p.15.

19 Anna Quinquaud's name can be found in Gordine's address book and she appears to have recommended the painter Anton Räderscheidt, who had shared her own studio in the rue des Plantes, as a tenant for Gordine's rue du Belvédère studio in Paris in October 1936 when Gordine had moved to London.

20 Borobudhur, the largest extant Buddhist temple complex, was built c. 750–830 CE by the Buddhist Sailendra Dynasty of Kings of south-central Java. It influenced the building and decoration of the temple complex at Angkor Wat, constructed in the early 12th century CE by the Hindu King Suryavarman II (reigned c. 1115–50 CE).

21 *Straits Times,* 12 August 1930, p.14.

22 See Black and Martin, Chapter One.

23 Shennan, for example, cites George Peel, the editor of the *Straits Times,* as commenting upon the widening gulf between the races attributable in part to the British and the 'professional Europeans' living in Malaya who showed no interest in the language or culture surrounding them. p.146.

24 15 August 1930: Meeting of Committee Number 4 of Singapore's Municipal Commissioners. The minutes show that Mr R. Braddell, a friend of Gordine's in London, suggested that 'an order be placed with Miss Gordine for some sculpture heads of Chinese, Indian and Malays for each of the hall landings in the Municipal Buildings.' Cited by Black, in Black and Martin pp.402–3.

25 When *Kwa Nin* was first exhibited in the UK, at the Leicester Galleries in July 1933, the critic Frank Rutter wrote that it was 'wonderful and well-nigh perfect in beauty of subject and treatment'. *Sunday Times,* 9 July 1933, p.7.

26 *Mongolian* and *Chinese* Head were installed on the second floor foyer of the Municipal Buildings, alongside a cast of the *Walking Male Torso,* while *Malay Head* and *Hindu Head* were on the first floor foyer, and in the board room, *Javanese Head.*

27 *Straits Times,* Saturday, 20 September 1930, p.10.

28 *Exhibition of Recent Sculpture and Drawings by Dora Gordine,* The Leicester Galleries, November 1938, p.6.

29 *Cingalese Girl,* for example, was included in the first Arts Council exhibition 'Open Air Sculpture' in Battersea Park, May–September 1948.

30 The photograph is reproduced in Black and Martin, p.67.

31 Allen, 2001, pp.149–51.

32 See Black and Martin, pp.123–24.

33 Dora Gordine, 'A Sense of Time', *The World Goes By,* BBC Home Service Radio, 6 January 1945, BBC Written Archives, Reading.

34 *Bangkok Times,* 21 February 1931.

35 *Straits Times,* 30 February 1930, p.12.

36 *Spectator,* 14 July 1933, pp.45–46.

37 *Spectator,* 4 November 1938, p.768.

38 See photograph of Gordine inside her studio at 21 Rue du Belvédère, Boulogne-Billancourt, Paris working on the figure of *Dyak,* c. March 1933.

39 *Morning Post,* 5 July 1933, p.6.

40 Janet Von Sternberg, *Fun in a Chinese Laundry* (London: Columbus Books, 1965), pp.77–78. He was in China in 1932 filming *Shanghai Express* with Marlene Dietrich.

41 Gordine, 'A Sense of Time', *The World Goes By,* BBC Home Service Radio, 6 January 1945, BBC Written Archives, Reading.

42 Hare to J.B. Manson, 24 September 1934, Manson Papers, HKRC, Tate, London.

43 Gordine, 'A Sense of Time'.

44 Keay, (London, 2005), pp.166–67.

45 Gordine, 'Beauty in the Home', *Not Only For Women,* BBC Far Eastern Service Radio, 18 April 1950, BBC Written Archives, Reading.

46 *Times,* 17 December 1940, p.5. Her lecture accompanied an exhibition of photographs of Indian sculpture and architecture at the Warburg Institute curated by Dr Stella Kramrisch (1896–1993), Lecturer in Indian Art at the Courtauld Institute of Art, London University.

47 *Times,* 3 January 1992, p.12.

CHAPTER THREE

1 *Straits Times of Singapore,* 12 August 1930, p.14.

2 Dora Gordine in the *Bangkok Times,* 21 February 1931, clipping, Archives, DHM.

3 'Dora Gordine Sculptures. Municipal Purchases', *Straits Times of Singapore,* 30 January 1931, p.12.

4 Black and Martin, 2007, p.241.

5 H.S. Goodhart-Rendel to Dora Gordine, 23 October 1937, Goodhart-Rendel Papers, Archives, RIBA, London.

6 Dora Gordine to H.S. Goodhart-Rendel, 1 November 1937, Goodhart-Rendel Papers, Archives, RIBA, London.

7 *Times,* 12 April 1938, p.12.

8 *Times,* 13 June 1931, p.14.

9 *Times,* 11 February 1938, p.11.

10 *Times,* 14 October 1938, p.16.

11 Annan, 1990, p.175 and Martin Pugh, *We Danced All Night: A Social History of Britain between the Wars* (London: The Bodley Head, 2008), p.137.

12 H.S. Goodhart-Rendel, 'Tribute to Mr Vanderpant', 7 November 1938, Goodhart-Rendel Papers, Archives, RIBA, London.

13 *Who Was Who: Volume V, 1951–1960* (London: 1953), p.1113.

14 *Times,* 26 November 1937, p.11.

15 Pugh, 2008, p.44.

16 Pugh, 2008, p.51.

17 *Times,* 28 February 1933, p.9.

18 *Times,* 21 May 1938, p.11.

19 Black and Martin, 2007, p.257.

20 *Yorkshire Evening Post,* 31 October 1938, clipping, Archives, DHM.

21 Dora Gordine in the *Surrey Comet,* 12 February 1955, clipping, Archives, DHM.

22 Dora Gordine to Muriel Orr-Ewing, undated (c. October 1946), University Archives, University of New York at Buffalo.

23 'Austerity' was a deliberate policy of curbing consumer spending very much associated with Sir Stafford Cripps, the Chancellor of the Exchequer in Clement Attlee's Labour Government. He was the husband of Gordine's friend Lady Isobel. David Kynaston, *Austerity Britain: 1945–51* (London: Bloomsbury, 2007), p.77.

24 Gordine, for example, lectured to the Royal Asiatic Society in May 1942 on 'The Sculpture of Indochina, Siam and Java' during which she discussed Khmer and Javanese depictions of the seated Buddha at length.

25 Kynaston, 2007, pp.85–86.

26 Dora Gordine to Muriel Orr-Ewing, undated (c. February 1947), Orr-Ewing Papers, University Archives, University of New York at Buffalo.

27 *Observer,* 16 March 1947, p.2.

28 J. Samson (Registrar of the Royal Society of the Arts) to Professor R.Y. Goodden, 5 May 1960, Archives, DHM.

29 Dora Gordine to J. Samson, 17 July 1960, Archives, DHM.

30 Press Release, Esso Petroleum, November 1960, Archives, DHM.

31 *Times,* 7 November 1960, p.7.

32 Tim Weiner, *Legacy of Ashes: The History of the CIA* (London: Penguin, 2008), pp.93–103.

33 Charlotte Curtis, 'Notes on England's Social Scene', *New York Times,* 22 July 1964, p.64.

34 Richard Hare to Josephine B. Jameson, 10 November 1960, Archives, Indianapolis Museum of Art.

35 *Connoisseur,* February 1961, p.44.

36 *Scotsman,* 31 October 1938, p.19 and Mary Sorrell, 'Dora Gordine', *Apollo,* May 1949, p.113.

37 *Times,* 21 May 1963, p.14.

38 Anna Pimlott-Baker, 'Sir David Smithers', H.C.G. Matthew & Brian Harrison, eds., *Oxford Dictionary of National Biography: Volume 61* (Oxford: Oxford University Press, 2004), pp.391–92.

CHRONOLOGY

Jonathan Black

8 June 1895: Dora Gordine born Dora Gordin in the Latvian port of Liepaja, then more commonly known as Libau, within the Russian Empire. Her father was Mark (also known as Morduch) Gordin, from a middle class Russian-Jewish background, and her mother Emma Esther née Schepshelewitch (1863/64–1930), from a Latvian-Jewish background. Dora had two elder brothers, Nikolai (1886–1941) and Leopold (1893–1979) and an elder sister, Anna (1892–1941).

1912–13: The Gordin family moved to live in the city of Reval (now known as Tallinn) in Estonia.

1915–16: Dora Gordin possibly studied sculpture at the National School of Applied Arts and Crafts, Tallinn.

February 1917: Russian Revolution in Petrograd/St. Petersburg. Tsar Nicholas II abdicated and the monarchy was shortly thereafter abolished.

April 1917: One of Dora Gordin's earliest known sculptures was exhibited at the Tallinn Cinema, Viru Tänav [Street].

25–26 October 1917: The Provisional Government of Alexander Kerensky was overthrown by the Bolsheviks.

November 1920: Dora Gordin exhibited a bronze portrait head with the 'ARS' Group at the Municipal Museum, Tallinn.

December 1921: Death of Mark/Morduch Gordin in mysterious circumstances in Latvia.

Autumn 1924: Gordin moved to Paris to continue her sculptural training.

April–May 1925: Employed as a mural painter in the British Pavilion at the Éxposition Internationale des Arts Décoratifis et Industriels Modernes in Paris.

May–August 1925: Exhibited, for the first time as 'Dora Gordine', a *Bronze* at the National Salon in Paris. She gave her nationality as 'Estonian' and her address as 'Maison des Étudiantes, 214 Boulevard Raspail'.

By the end of 1925 she had met the celebrated sculptor Aristide Maillol (1861–1944). Gordine later claimed her was impressed by her work and advised her not to continue her sculptural training at an art school: 'Work where you can, and how you can, but work alone.'

Early 1926: Introduced to Janet Vaughan (1899–1993) by David Gourlay – co-owner of the Wayfarers Travel Agency which had an office in Paris. Gordine often stayed with Vaughan, then a medical student, in her room at 19 Taviton Street, Bloomsbury. Later that same year Vaughan introduced Gordine to the Honourable Richard Hare (1907–66), second son of the 4th Earl of Listowel and then a student at Balliol College, Oxford. Hare quickly asked Gordine to marry him but she refused because she first wanted to establish herself as a successful sculptor.

May–June 1926: Encouraged by the established sculptors François Pompon (1855–1933) and Antoine Bourdelle (1861–1929) Gordine exhibited two bronzes at the Salon des Tuileries, Paris: *Head of a Chinaman* (later known as *The Chinese Philosopher*) and *Torso*. Both works were cast by the prestigious Valsuani Foundry at 74 rue des Plantes. She continued to use Valsuani for the next thirteen years.

August 1928: Gordine left the Gordin family home, 4 Narva Boulevard, Tallinn, to live full-time in Paris.

October 1928: Gordine exhibited 17 bronzes, alongside the painter C.R.W. Nevinson, at the Leicester Galleries, Leicester Square, London. The exhibition was both a commercial and critical success.

1929–30: The celebrated French architect Auguste Perret (1874–1954) built Gordine a stylish modernist studio-home at 21 Rue du Belvédère in Boulogne-Billancourt, south-west Paris.

September–October 1929: Gordine exhibited sixteen bronzes with two German painters, Fritz Kronenberg (1901–60) and Paul Strecker (1898–1950), at the Galérie Alfred Flechtheim, Berlin.

November–December 1929: Gordine's bronzes *Breton Head* and *Mongolian Head* were included in the exhibition 'Modern and African Sculpture' at the Sydney Burney Gallery, 13 St. James's Place, London. Other exhibitors included Maillol, Ossip Zadkine, Jacob Epstein, Barbara Hepworth, John Skeaping and Frank Dobson, alongside carvings from the Ivory Coast, Gabon, Nigeria, Benin and the Congo.

January 1930: Gordine arrived in Singapore. She then moved to live in the town of Johor Bahru, capital of the Unfederated Malay State of Johor.

August 1930: The Singapore Municipal Commissioners invited Gordine to provide six bronzes for the interior of the recently completed Municipal Buildings – now the Old Parliament Building, Singapore.

18 September 1930: Married Dr George Herbert Garlick (1886–1958), then Deputy Chief Medical Officer of the Johor Medical Service, at the Singapore Registry Office. On the marriage licence Gordine stated she was born in 1898.

January–March 1931: Gordine travelled through Malaya, the Dutch East Indies, French Indo-China (Cambodia) and Thailand.

September–October 1932: Dora Gordine moved into 21 rue du Belvédère, Boulogne-Billancourt.

July 1933: Exhibited 15 bronzes at the Leicester Galleries, London, alongside the American painter Edward Bruce.

October 1933: Gordine returned to Johor via Paris.

Autumn 1934: Gordine visited Java, Bali, French Indo-China and then Shanghai and Beijing.

July 1935: Gordine arrived in London, from Singapore, and began divorce proceedings against Dr Garlick.

September 1935: Richard Hare, on Gordine's behalf, purchased a plot of land on Kingston Hill on which a house she had largely designed would be built. The house will be called 'Dorich House' – a composite of Dora and Richard.

2 November 1936: Gordine's divorce from Dr Garlick became absolute.

6 November 1936: Gordine married Richard Hare at the Chelsea Registry Office. Shortly thereafter they moved into Dorich House. On the marriage licence Gordine stated she was a 'spinster' and gave the year of her birth as 1906.

April 1938: Gordine elected an Associate Member of the Royal Society of British Sculpture (RBS) along with Frank Dobson, Eric Gill, Thomas Huxley-Jones and Maurice Lambert.

May 1938: H.S.E. Vanderpant presented Gordine's bronze *Seated Baby*, which he commissioned, to the Westminster City Council Maternity and Child Welfare Centre and Day Nursery on Bessborough Street, London, SW1.

November 1938: Exhibition at the Leicester Galleries comprising 30 bronzes and 21 drawings.

November 1938: Gordine appeared twice that month in the BBC Television Programme *Picture Page*.

September 1939: Shortly after the outbreak of the Second World War, Richard Hare joined the Ministry of Information.

December 1940: Gordine lectured in London to the Royal Asiatic Society on 'The Beauty of Asiatic Sculpture'.

January 1942: Gordine made an unsuccessful attempt to obtain an official war artist appointment from the War Artists Advisory Committee (WAAC) of the Ministry of Information and be elected an Associate of the Royal Academy (ARA).

March 1942: Richard Hare appointed Senior Assistant Specialist to the Anglo-Soviet Relations Division of the Ministry of Information.

May 1942: Gordine lectured to the Royal Asiatic Society on 'The Indonesian Sculpture of Indo-China and Java' at the Royal Empire Society Building, London.

March 1944: Richard Hare was promoted to become Deputy Head of the Anglo-Soviet Relations Division at the Ministry of Information.

September 1944: Lectured on 'Indian Sculpture' for the Royal India Society and on 'Chinese Sculpture' for the Royal Asiatic Society, London.

January 1945: Gordine gave a radio broadcast on 'A Sense of Time' for the BBC Home Service programme *The World Goes By*.

May 1945: Richard Hare was promoted to become Director of the Anglo-Soviet Relations Division at the Ministry of Information.

October–November 1945: Exhibited 28 pieces of sculpture (25 bronzes, 2 plasters and 1 in silver pewter) at the Leicester Galleries.

March 1946: Richard Hare left the Ministry of Information.

May 1946: Gordine's bronze low-relief portrait of Sun Yat-sen (1866–1925), first President of the Chinese Republic, unveiled in Warwick Court, Gray's Inn Place, London.

October 1947–September 1948: Visited the United States with Richard Hare – who had been awarded a one-year Fellowship by the Rockefeller Foundation, to develop 'Slavic Studies' at the Hoover Institute, Stanford University, California. Gordine lived for a while in Los Angeles, developed contacts within Hollywood and gave several lectures on sculpture to women's groups.

November 1948: Discussed her sculpture on the BBC Television programme *Designed for Women*.

January 1949: Appeared again on BBC Television.

February 1949: Gordine was nominated for election as an Associate of the Royal Academy but did not receive a single vote.

May–September 1949: Contributed work to the first Arts Council exhibition 'Open Air Sculpture' in Battersea Park.

September 1949: Richard Hare appointed a lecturer in Russian literature at the School of Slavonic Studies (later SSEES), London University.

October 1949: Gordine elected a Fellow of the RBS.

November 1949: Exhibited 32 pieces of sculpture (31 bronzes and 1 plaster) at the Leicester Galleries, London. This was Gordine's last solo exhibition.

January 1950: Gordine gave a radio broadcast 'Sculpture and Everyday Life' for the BBC Home Service programme *Mainly for Women*.

June–September 1951: Gordine's *Male Torso* (*Dyak*) was exhibited at the Festival of Britain.

June 1951: Sold her studio-house in Paris, at 21 Rue du Belvédère, for 300,000 francs.

November–December 1953: First Exhibition of the Society of Portrait Sculptors (SPS), Imperial Institute Art Gallery, London. Gordine was a founder member of the Society along with: Gilbert Ledward, Charles Wheeler, Jacob Epstein and Frank Dobson. She exhibited annually with the SPS until 1959.

February 1956: A final and also unsuccessful attempt to be elected an ARA.

February 1957: Elected a Fellow of the Royal Society for the Encouragement of Arts.

February–June 1959: Visited Bloomington, Indiana with Richard Hare who had been appointed a temporary Visiting Professor in the Department of Slavic Languages and Literature at Indiana University.

May 1960: Gordine exhibited for the last time at the Royal Academy, London.

November 1960: Bronze low-relief *Power* unveiled, by the Duke of Edinburgh, in the Administrative Block of the new Esso Petroleum Refinery at Milford Haven.

Spring 1962: Richard Hare appointed Professor of Russian literature at SSEES, London University.

May 1963: Bronze group *Mother and Child* unveiled by Queen Elizabeth II in the entrance foyer of the Royal Marsden Cancer Hospital, Sutton, Surrey.

October 1964: A second cast of *Mother and Child* unveiled in the entrance hall of the Indianapolis Museum of Art, Indiana, USA.

September 1966: Richard Hare died at Dorich House from a heart attack. He left his wife £33,000 in his will.

August 1977: Gordine ceased casting work with the Morris Singer Foundry.

May 1981: *Guadeloupe Head* included in 'British Sculpture in the Twentieth Century', Whitechapel Art Gallery.

June–August 1986: *Chinese Philosopher*, *Kwa Nin* (*Chinese Lady of Peace*) and *Malay Sultana* exhibited in 'Sculpture in Britain between the Wars', Fine Art Society, London.

29 December 1991: Gordine died at Dorich House from a stroke.

May–August 2004: *Guadeloupe Head*; *Mongolian Head*; *Malay Sultana* and *Javanese Head* exhibited in 'Head to Head', Tate Modern, London.

February 2004: Dorich House awarded Museum Status by Resource: The Council for Museums, Archives and Libraries.

January–May 2006: Exhibition *Embracing the Exotic: Jacob Epstein and Dora Gordine* held at the Ben Uri Gallery, the London Jewish Museum of Art, and the Hatton Gallery, University of Newcastle.

February 2008: Publication of monograph *Dora Gordine: Sculptor, Artist, Designer* by Jonathan Black and Brenda Martin (Philip Wilson Publishers, London).

February–May 2009: Major Retrospective Exhibition *Dora Gordine: Sculptor, Artist, Designer* held at Dorich House Museum, Kingston University and the Kingston Museum, Kingston upon Thames, Surrey.

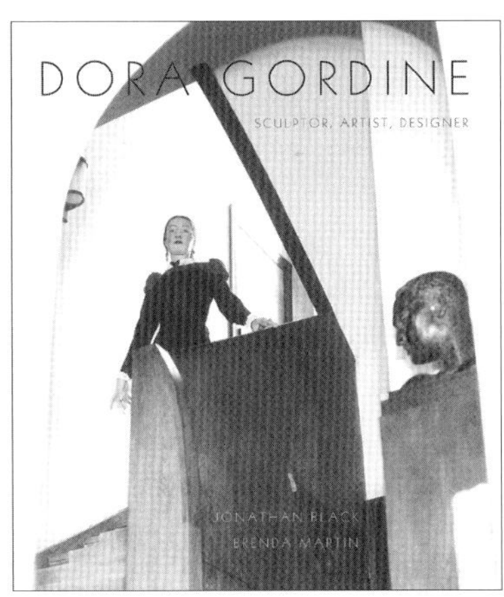

272 pages
275 x 235 mm
28 colour and
204 monochrome illustrations
Hardback
ISBN 978-0-85667-644-4

DORA GORDINE
SCULPTOR, ARTIST, DESIGNER

In 1938 Dora Gordine was hailed by a leading contemporary critic as someone who would shortly become 'the finest woman sculptor in the world'. She was widely perceived as a major presence in European sculpture for over thirty years, recognised for her contribution to the interwar art movement known as the Rappel à l'Ordre, and was a prominent member of the Royal Society of British Sculptors and a founder of the Society of Portrait Sculptors. As a sculptor, she was widely admired as a creator of psychologically acute portrait heads, distinctive public memorials and sensuous figure sculpture. However, her highly individual sense of style, evident in the studio homes she had built for herself in Paris, Singapore and London, also repays attention. The last of these homes, Dorich House, which is located on the edge of Richmond Park and is the most architecturally intriguing of the three, was designed by Gordine herself, a feat virtually unheard of at the time of its construction in 1936.

Gifted, charismatic, imperious and irrepressible, Gordine has appeared to many as something of an enigma, and this is perhaps not surprising given her eagerness to foster the air of uncertainty that surrounded her background, nationality and age. This book is the first to uncover the reality of her colourful life, containing a wealth of previously unpublished material, as well as providing a comprehensive assessment of her undoubted achievements as both a talented and versatile sculptor, and an artist who possessed a distinct flair for architectural and interior design. Richly illustrated with ample colour plates and monochrome illustrations – many of which are published here for the first time – the book also contains the first catalogue raisonné of Gordine's impressive oeuvre.

'[A] handsome and well-illustrated book [with evidence of] a remarkable amount of sleuthing.' – *The Art Newspaper*

'[A] handsome and well-illustrated production [that] makes a significant contribution to broader debates on sculpture in the inter-war period.' – *The Art Book, USA*